EXPERTS, BRAIN SCIENCE

"People do change, yet not by using traditional change management strategies. Reut has done an incredible job of debunking the myths leaders hold about change and then providing a system based on moving people into action quickly. The Art and Science of Changing People who don't Want to Change doesn't focus on what managers need to say. It shares practical steps on what to do to grow your organization today." **Dr. Marcia Reynolds**, PsyD, author of *Outsmart Your Brain: How to Make Success Feel Easy*

"Reut Schwartz-Hebron has done an excellent job addressing organizational myths and examining how people actually change. She has woven together insights from organizational psychology, coherent management practices, and neuroscience into an insightful book that is a must read for managers in organizations." **John B. Arden**, PhD., author of *Rewire Your Brain*

"Reut Schwartz-Hebron takes a basic insight of applied brain plasticity — the fact that the brain requires experience in order to encode and manifest directed change — and shows how to use this principle in a systematic way to create change in an organizational setting. This book presents a very clear, pragmatic and user-friendly approach to making brain change into a genuinely effective real world human process." **Jeffrey M. Schwartz** MD Research Psychiatrist, UCLA School of Medicine and author of *You Are Not Your Brain*

EXPERTS, TEAM AND BUSINESS DEVELOPMENT

"Interesting, compelling, and fact-based, this work has the right blend of stories, illustrations, and brain-science to keep readers engaged throughout. Leaders and their teams will have a clear understanding of how to achieve new ways of getting results and clearly know why they are doing it. Reut effectively confronts the reality of "change" head on. She breaks through the myths that perpetuate ineffective change initiatives at organizations and provides clear strategies and passageways for real results. What a comprehensive and masterful work! I will be recommending this book!" **Tom Schulte**, Executive Director of Linked 2 Leadership and CEO of Recalibrate Professional Development

"This book will change how you think about change. The immediately applicable strategies in this book will help business leaders become the change agents their organizations need to survive in this ever-changing world." **Ronald M. Katz**, president, Penguin Human Resource Consulting and author of *Someone's Gonna Get Hired...It Might As Well Be You!*

"The old adage 'a leopard can't change its spots' may be in for a change itself after you read Reut Schwartz-Hebron's new book *Changing People Who Don't Want To Change*. Schwartz-Hebron's experience, backed by detailed research, blows up the myths about change and offers key strategies you can use today to create the environment you need for success. Whether you are a change agent or an in-the-trenches leader, you'll want to keep this reference close by. Read it today and change your tomorrows." **Robert H. Thompson**, author of *The Offsite: A Leadership Challenge Fable*

"Thank you Reut! A brilliant work that brings science into the amorphous task of motivating and changing behaviors in the work place. This book hits a home run in debunking the myths associating with changing people, and gives the reader a blueprint for their own implementation. Well done, must read for any leader looking to maximize team performance." **Judy Hissong**, Principal, Nesso Strategies

"This is a must read book for anyone! The integration of the inner workings of teams in addition to many of the most prevalent myths we have about change allows readers to experience a first-hand self-reflection to better understand the evolution of change and key strategies for successful change. Reut's hidden gems are the 'Chapter Takaways' which give readers valuable and concise memorable insights." **Dr. Michael C. Pickett**, author of *Ethical Leadership: Leadership for a New Millennium*

"This book is a gifted combination of theory, research, and storytelling. The takeaways provide quick and solid reference for the reader to self evaluate. As the author says, 'Change is the soul of business excellence.' It appeals to the different ways people learn and helps them understand the need for fear-free change." **Kelly Karius**, author of *This is Out of Control! A Practical Guide to Managing Conflicts*

"Change doesn't come easy for most people, including business people. In today's environment, constant change has become the norm, moving stress levels and resistance to change to new heights. This book not only identifies the most common teams facing change, their characteristics and attributes, but key strategies designed to help them adapt to changes they would normally resist. As study of the human brain and neuroscience advance and are incorporated into business situations, Reut's processes create excellent paths to success." **Terri L Maurer**, author of *Interior Design in Practice: Case Studies of Successful Business Models*

"The dark ages of witchdoctors and voodoo psychology are now over. Much like a single beam of brilliance shining in through the murky depths of the sciences studying human behavior, author Schwartz-Hebron nails it. Change doesn't require open-brain surgery, just the simple techniques found in this book. Having read this, the world to me, is now a better place." Futurist **Thomas Frey**, Executive Director of the DaVinci Institute.

"While most humans alive would agree that nothing in life gets better by chance — they only get better by change — we seem to be wired to resist the very thing that will help us progress! Implementing change in organizations is almost always difficult as a result and Reut's book gives leaders science-based insights which not only support employees — but also ensure the required changes are pervasively made. Since change is constant in business, leaders need to read this book." **Mark C. Crowley**, author of *Lead From The Heart: Transformational Leadership For The 21st Century*

"An intriguing examination of how the way the brain works can influence behavioral change in teams. The book builds step-by-step to a science-based but user-friendly method of creating change in people who resist change (virtually all of us!). It is a worthwhile read and useful addition to the thoughtful manager's library." **Eric Flamholtz**, Professor Emeritus of Management, Anderson School, UCLA and President, Management Systems Consulting Corporation

"Reut Schwartz-Hebron has pioneered a new approach to change management in business, a system that is based upon recent findings in neuroscience, as well as on extensive experience. I was personally happy to see Ms. Schwartz-Hebron's incorporation of brain science findings as the basis for this new approach, as I know from my own research over the past ten years how ground-breaking the findings have been and to what extent they have been transforming our understanding of how our minds operate and what drives behavior." **Diane Brandon**, Creativity/Intuition Teacher, Intuitive Consultant, and author of *Invisible Blueprints*

"Changing people, cultures, and organizations is hard — especially for people who don't want to change! Reut introduces a scientific way to facilitate positive changes, optimize your potential, and reach your goals. She shares real-world business examples throughout the book. The concepts, processes and strategies are simple and powerful, and can be applied to all aspects of life! Not only does the book change how you will incorporate change at your company, but it changes you as well!" **Kevin Karschnik**, Director of Training at iSpeak, Inc., speaker and Co-author of *Corporate Ovations: Reaching New Heights by Reaching Your Audience*

"Lots of people write books about change. Lots of people claim to understand the dynamics of change. Most of these people are rehashing old ideas about how and why we change. This book is well-researched, well-organized, and well-written and deserves to be read and reread by anyone who works with people who are in or will face the challenge of effective change." **John E. Smith**, MA; The Strategic Learning Group LLC

"This book is definitely required reading for those that want to accomplish great things in this world. Leading people well through changes within an organization is an inevitable and re-occurring situation that often goes poorly and drains too many resources. But now we have a new set of tools to remedy this! Reut's perspective, science and proven tools are indispensible to both the novice and well-seasoned leader alike." **Joon S. Han**, Leading business strategist and author of *Get Ahead by Giving Back*

"Reut does a marvelous job challenging conventional change wisdom with real-life examples supported by neuroscientific strategies. I am looking forward to integrating these ideas into my own teaching and practice." **Dr. Jeffrey R. Mueller**, President, JRM Enterprises

"Change is hard, and sometimes feels impossible, but Reut has provided a roadmap for leaders to influence change in their organization

— even with those tough-to-reach people who don't think change is necessary. With real actionable tools that change the way leaders inspire and influence their people, this book is a must read for anyone striving to build a high performance work environment in their organization." **Bill Hogg**, Organizational Transformation & Performance Excelerator™ and Board Member Canadian Association of CAPS Toronto

"After 27 years of helping companies large and small implement strategic change, this is the first book I have read that presents a compelling case for how individuals and teams respond to change and provides strategies to facilitate change in the common scenarios presented. A well-written, easily-read book complete with theory, anecdotes, and strategies that is a worthwhile read for any manager or consultant responsible for helping organizations change." **John Bryan**, DBA, CMC, President, eProcesses Consulting and Adjunct Professor, Grand Canyon University College of Doctoral Studies

"Reut Schwartz-Hebron's new book is a must read for every leader dealing with today's constant barrage of changing technology, systems, and markets. This fresh approach combines time-tested change management practices with practical applications of the latest brain and behavior science — the result is a powerful approach to creating sustainable change. Reut, thank you for this great handbook! It belongs on every leader's desktop!" **Ron Black**, Founder, The Mentor Group

EXECUTIVES

"There is magic in this book. As someone who used this system I felt it was like turning on the switch, giving you access to abilities you didn't know you had. This system was developed by one of the most brilliant minds I know and it will impact your life. Written in an easy-to-read format with well-defined steps, it is a treasure for organizations and managers everywhere." **Carey Harrington Adolfsson**, CEO, Diagnostic and Defense Technology Analysts

"Change as science? – What a concept! This book presents current brain science, explains exactly why the same old model of defining and focusing on desired outcomes and ignoring resistance to change is a dead end. We learn why the ever so sought after "Aha moment" is not the Holy Grail after all! Pardon the pun though I must say that implanting

Reut's process is a 'no brainer' in not only achieving true and lasting organizational change in mere weeks but also ultimately gifting teams with the ability to change themselves!" **Kathleen Fouts**, SPHR-CA

"How fast can organizations adapt to a changing world? Innovative teams need change strategies that really work. Reut Schwartz-Hebron unlocks the barriers to real transformation. This book leads us through a new approach that is perfectly on target for our rapidly changing times. This insightful system harnesses research from brain science to create new pathways to success. Prepare to be inspired." **Cece O'Connor**, Principle Innovator, Experience Strategy

"Through this book, Ms. Schwartz Hebron has potentially provided the tools to influence human interactions more positively and completely than any other observer of human behavior. This work is truly a game-changer and a must read." **F. Nicholas Jacobs**, International Director, SunStone Consulting and previous President of Windber Medical Center and the Windber Research Institute

"Rapid and effective change is the key to business survival in what has become the most competitive global business environment we have seen. Change has truly become the new steady state. It has never been more important than now as a leader to unlock the tools and strategies to have the ability to nurture sustainable and lasting change. I have leveraged the program and have personally witnessed the amazing results." **Greg Flickinger** Ph.D, Vice President of Manufacturing and Corporate Engineering at Snyder's-Lance Inc.

"This methodology of inspiring change is simply brilliant. Utilizing neurological studies and years of practice, Reut delivers a simple and sure way of creating change, far away from traditional strategies. This is the future of organizational development and change practices. I highly recommend exploring this masterpiece. Reut is a true thought leader in the field of change today." Dena Ayala, Division Manager, Suna Solutions

"This is an intriguing read that provides a deeper understanding of the dynamics in getting people to change. It does so by unveiling the truths about change and providing a systematic approach to acquiring, overcoming, and applying key strategies that the brain accepts as superior to previous beliefs." **Andrea Watson**, Vendor Relations Manager, Warner Bros. Entertainment, Inc.

THE ART AND SCIENCE OF CHANGING PEOPLE WHO DON'T WANT TO CHANGE

FORWARD BY MARSHALL GOLDSMITH

THINKERS50 LEADERSHIP AWARD WINNER:
RECOGNIZED AS THE #1 LEADERSHIP THINKER IN THE WORLD

Giving Teams Access To Their Full Potential

©Reut Schwartz-Hebron
Key Change Institute
JANUARY 2012

Published by Real House Press, San Diego, California.

For information about permission to reproduce selections from this book,
write to Permissions, Real House Press 14255 Manzella St. San Diego
California 92129

Ordering Information
Quantity sales. Special discounts are available on quantity purchases by
corporations, associations, and others. For details contact "Special Sales
Department" at info@KeyChangeNow.com

Real House Press and the RHP logo are registered trademarks of Real
House Press.

Cover and layout design: Justine Elliott
Editing and Ghostwriting: Kristen James
Library of Congress Cataloging-in-Publication Data
Reut Schwartz-Hebron., 1973
The Art and Science of Changing People who don't Want to change /
Reut Schwartz-Hebron
Includes references
ISBN: 978-0-9799394-3-3

Printed in the United States of America
First edition

★

This book is dedicated to my family.
Without them I would not have had the
privilege of reinforcing the synaptic pathways
that are aligned with my core.

CONTENTS

FOREWORD

BY MARSHALL GOLDSMITH

With *The Art and Science of Changing People Who Don't Want to Change*, Reut Schwartz-Hebron delves into fascinating research about the systems in the brain related to change. Reut explores how solutions can be designed that will influence people to make modifications that will guide the organization and/or team to achieve results.

This book comes at a critical time when major organizations must navigate increasingly rapid and global change. Teams are becoming more critical and important to organizational success. Leaders are finding themselves members of all kinds of teams, from virtual teams to autonomous, cross-functional teams and action-learning teams. How do leaders navigate through common challenges their companies face?

The challenges that Reut covers in this book, such as stimulating innovation and differentiation, creating long-term value, and executing strategy consistently, are faced by leaders every day. And often the result is not success. As

Reut stresses, the need to build effective teams is critical, and the necessity of building teams in an environment of rapid change with limited resources, increased demand, and fewer staff members is common.

The interesting focus and unique solution offered in *The Art and Science of Changing People Who Don't Want to Change* is a process for making adjustments, which is dependent on your type of team. Is your team a Doubtful Analyst, Emotional Oscillator, Pleasing, Flamboyant, or Stability Team? With this diagnosis, Reut reveals a design of a five-stage process that will take your team to the next level in business, and perhaps even help team members make positive adjustments throughout their lives.

The Art and Science of Changing People Who Don't Want to Change is one of those rare books that you'll want to take to heart, read it, study it, share it with your team. The more time you invest in this process, the greater the return for your team and your organization!

....

MARSHALL GOLDSMITH is the Thinkers50 Leadership Award Winner – for the World's Most-Influential Leadership Thinker. He is the million-selling author of 31 books, including New York Times bestsellers, *MOJO* and *What Got You Here Wont' Get You There.*

INTRODUCTION

When asked if they are willing to change or make needed adjustments at work, most people answer yes. Most people genuinely want to make adjustments that will benefit them personally and their organization. When it comes down to it though, only 10% of people will apply changes and make needed adjustments in a lasting way.[1]

If we want to simplify things, we can say that the world can be divided into three categories of people: those who can easily change and adjust, those who believe they want to change, but are unable to change, and those who get stuck and resist making needed adjustments. The first category of people who can change includes only 10% of people. The focus of this book is on the other 90%. It's about changing people who cannot or will not make the needed adjustments required in order for your organization to access its full potential. Now, it's not about us against them, and they

---

1   HRIQ worldwide survey, *Leading Global Change: Best Practices Report,* People NRG Publication, 2011

are not stubborn, uncaring people. People need certain circumstances to change, and this book unlocks a system that makes these circumstances possible.

In today's fast-paced global business environment, the need for mergers, acquisitions, downsizing, or fast growth, is inevitable. People are constantly required to make adjustments. Change is the soul of business excellence. In the 21st century, prosperity, and success can only come from constantly applying the next level of change. There is no growth without change. Knowing how to get people to acquire the changes they need to make, especially in business, is a new and growing area of expertise.

Business schools prepare people to manage systems. There are excellent models for marketing, project management, strategy and other such areas, but with people the challenge is slightly different. The brilliant models for decision making, problem solving, or communication are not enough without a system that will get people in organizations to adopt those and other models in a lasting way.

You probably hear a lot about better results and better tools, how company X has achieved its success or which values are common in the top 2% of businesses. But so far most organizations have not been able to adopt ideal models or even follow their own best practices because, until now, a system that would get people to put those models into practice has been missing.

This book focuses on such a system and on how it's applied to specific teams. More specifically, it explores how good teams are at changing and making needed adjustments.

PART ONE
GIVING YOU ACCESS TO
YOUR TEAM'S POTENTIAL

You may think only difficult people don't want to change. Studies show that in reality most people don't want to change. While 81% of professionals say "yes" to change only approximately 10% then take action to support it.[2]

Let's face it: people are creatures of habit and change means we have to re-adjust. This explains why 70% of mergers and acquisitions lose shareholder value[3]. In fact, 68% of IT projects fail[4] because leaders don't have access to solutions that will get people to make needed adjustments. It's why most training fades away within 6 weeks.[5] Put all together, people who don't want to change cost businesses at least $1 trillion, perhaps as much as $3 trillion a year worldwide.

---

2 HRIQ worldwide survey, *Leading Global Change: Best Practices Report*, People NRG Publication, 2011
3 KPMG Global Survey, *A New Dawn: Good Deals in Challenging Times*, May 2011
4 Standish Group report, CHAOS Summary, April 2009
5 John T. Wixted and Ebbe B. Ebbesen, *On the Form of Forgetting*, American Psychological Society Vol. 2, November 1991

If successful, changing people who don't want to change or who can't seem to change ranks as a top investment with very high ROI. But, as you know from experience, it's extremely difficult to do. This is why you're reading this book, and why I wrote it.

I plan to change how you incorporate change.

Within every business problem is a people problem. The way people learn, plan, interact and execute is at the heart of almost any business success or failure.

When people struggle to change, it undermines, deters, or even sinks the organization's ability to compete, adapt, and innovate. Imagine what you could accomplish if you could get people to change, and not just the difficult few. Imagine the potential if you could get teams to make the needed adjustments that would lead to desired outcomes.

The answer is not to charm, prod, or manipulate. The solution is to gift teams with the right conditions, allowing them to adjust in a lasting way. It permanently changes the way people react, expands people's ability to cope, cooperate, and resourcefully tackle your organization's biggest challenges.

Part One is about a new solution that shows you what is now possible thanks to scientific developments. I'll explore the myths that have been holding you back from being able to change people, even people who don't want to change.

A NEW WAY

There is a better way to optimize your organization's potential and achieve goals.

As the VP of sales in a pharmaceuticals company that just underwent a merger, Steve had much to worry about. Last week he finalized his team and tried to encourage them, but his words still echoed in his head: "The next few weeks are going to be difficult, but now that we're past the most difficult part of the merger, we'll be able to work through anything in our way."

He knew it was something he was supposed to say. Deep down he wanted to believe it. But the truth was he doubted they were over the hard part. He had people on the team who didn't trust him, people who struggled with new products they had to promote, and everyone had adjustments to make. His experience taught him the team would start feeling the full weight of the merger in the next few months, and he knew it wasn't going to be easy.

Mergers and acquisitions are among the most researched

and planned events in business. There's plenty at stake. The value of global acquisitions is greater than the Gross Domestic Product of all but the top 10% of the world's economies. Though these investments receive great attention, studies show more than 70% of mergers and acquisitions lose shareholder value and 75% are considered unsuccessful by key stakeholders.

Despite an apparently thorough "due diligence" process, many mergers and acquisitions still fail to meet pre-merger objectives. That's not a valuation problem; it's a people problem.

The people factor, and especially people's ability to adjust and effectively respond to new organizational needs, often determines the success or failure of strategic initiatives.

WHAT'S GOING ON HERE?

Steve's experience leading his sales department through a merger is a very common one. *"Imagine having to sell your biggest rival's competing products. In this industry our sales force understands change is inevitable but some of our people can't just switch off what they feel. They didn't want this to happen. The biggest risk right now is losing top talent and somehow I also need to keep sales up...I realize this is complicated but I can't be their nanny; they are just going to have to cope with it but at the same time I really don't want to lose them."* VP of Sales, pharmaceutical industry

People who don't want to change are not a rare few individuals. Most people, a majority of the people in your organization, will not make desired adjustments to meet business needs without the right system in place.

Even when people understand how important the change is and when they believe the change is needed, most people will not be able to make needed adjustments and change in a lasting way.

Not wanting to change is so prevalent that even 90% of heart attack victims go back to their old diets and sedentary behaviors 6 months later. No doubt, regardless of your age, industry, profession, or nationality, you have personal experiences dealing with people who don't want to change.

Steve's case, where people got in the way of increased productivity, is one example of the elusive forces blocking organizations from accessing their full potential.

Businesses of all sizes invest billions each year to train and develop people. In the US alone, businesses spend more than 300 billion dollars yearly to enhance people's productivity[6]. Yet, studies measuring the transference from training indicate that little of this investment in people transfers into effective execution.

When people don't change or adjust in a way matching the needs and goals of the business, it's impossible for organizations to access optimal productivity.

People tend to be an organization's greatest expense, but they also produce the revenue, productivity, innovation, and competitive advantages. The human factor is the single most important variable for making a quantum leap in results.

Tapping into that potential has proven to be problematic. Steve had to cope with extreme resistance. His team, like most teams in similar situations, blocked Steve and the organization as a whole from having access to higher revenue and productivity.

If you are dissatisfied with a 10%-30% success rate from development and change efforts, doesn't it make sense to consider a new approach? Isn't it reasonable to believe more adaptive and innovative workforce is the kind of change that

---

6   Gallup, Employee Engagement: *A Leading Indicator of Financial Performance*, www.Gallup.com

would produce a leap in performance? Doesn't there have to be a better way?

MAKING THE LEAP

The reality of the 21st century is change from technology, regulations, global competition, and innovation is relentless. People are frequently experiencing forced change simply because change is imperative for the survival and success of business.

It took 10 years of ground-breaking development and refinement to discover how to empower you to access your team's potential, optimize productivity, and increase the success of business investments. This book is about a new and better way. Leaders will gain access to better results. Organizations will learn to access their full potential by helping people across the organization apply needed adjustments in a rewarding and lasting way. For the first time, there is a way to equip you with a system for changing people, especially those who don't want to change or seem to be unable to change.

For Steve, using this new way meant equipping his sales teams to adjust to a difficult change like a merger, so they could achieve goals without feeling forced. *"The brilliance of this system is it prepares you to get people to change, with cooperation, even when they don't want to change, can't seem to be able to change or when they don't know they need to change. I was very honest and direct with my team and it helped a lot to know which type of skills we needed as a team. I was able to guide my team to results, without compromising my expectations. It's difficult, but just because we are going through this merger doesn't mean we can afford to leave our sales goals unmet. As a result of this process the team responded very well to the change. We gave them tools to achieve what we demanded of them."* VP of Sales, pharmaceutical industry

The key to a successful merger transaction is effective integration of two companies, products, channels, technology, clients, and people into a single business unit, capable of achieving new goals. Almost every step taken during a merger is in some way or another associated with forcing change on people or forcing people out of their comfort zone.

Helping people become more adaptive not only is a competitive advantage, it's also humane. Low morale, illness from stress, and workplace violence are real problems too. By equipping people to make needed changes and adjustments you are creating a genuine win-win situation that benefits the organization as much as it supports people.

There is a new way, a system that equips managers and teams with a concrete toolkit to overcome needed challenges and directly to achieve desired outcomes. Instead of depending mostly on communications and trying to minimize resistance, this new system targets and expands people's capacity to change and adjust.

Instead of ignoring the inability to change, the system in this book makes it the main focus.

The focus of this book is application. A system that gets people unstuck, giving the organization access to optimal productivity and desired outcomes.

NEW THINKING

Mergers are an obvious extreme, but people are forced to change all the time in business. Sometimes you'll see it when people don't acquire new behaviors, apply new regulations, or adopt a new system. It affects little things, like completing forms incorrectly or reaching vital goals, like reorganizations, successful product launches, and retaining and satisfying your best customers.

The impact of the inability to change is far reaching, perhaps more than you realize. In fact, sometimes leaders are hindered by their own inability to change and aren't aware of it.

Bill has been with the company for over 20 years. As a COO in the manufacturing industry, he could see the company plunge during the economic downturn. After that the owners decided to get re-involved. Bill believed that the owners taking back control wasn't the needed solution at this stage of the business. *"The most important thing right now is to redefine roles in a way that serves our sales efforts. I can understand the need to be involved as an owner...we need to serve the business with our strengths starting with looking at things soberly."* COO, manufacturing industry

During the slow economy, the owners of the large, family-owned corporation, took back managing the company, especially marketing and sales. The rest of the leadership team believed this change wasn't the best use of the owners' talents. In fact, the leadership team brought up their concerns with the owners several times. It seemed like the owners were uncomfortable stepping away from these critical functions and were not ready to risk leaving these critical roles to anyone else. The dynamics in the leadership team and the difference in perspectives made it impossible for the organization to optimize productivity. This dynamic blocked the leadership team from reaching business goals and accessing the organization's full potential.

It's very common for leaders in the organization to be unaware of the fact they themselves don't want to change. Many times teams cannot effectively discuss needed improvements because those needs require senior leadership to make changes and adjustments. When this happens, the organization doesn't have access to the knowledge that will lead to the right decisions for the organization as a whole.

In Bill's organization, the dynamics in the leadership team didn't allow the organization to maximize strengths and minimize weaknesses. The value of leadership interactions was not optimized, and as a result, choices made by the leadership team didn't serve a clear path to specific business goals.

Equipping the leadership as a whole with the ability to change people who don't want to change made it possible for the team to develop a clear, effective discussion and reach needed conclusions with cooperation and agreement.

Equipping the organization's leadership with a new way to solve an old problem made an important difference. Bill attributed the success to building a common perspective: *"Our success was a great breakthrough in communication and cooperation. Going in, we each had our own perspective on what should change, but the targeted approach of the process gave us, as a team, the specific keys we needed in order to agree and design the right solution."* COO, manufacturing industry

To successfully change other people requires overcoming many traps, one of which is overcoming the power that habits and repetition have on people.

The power of habits will often fail even the most willing and cooperative team from acquiring change.

Most people will not apply needed change, regardless of their attitude.

Frequently people will be more than happy to invest time and energy in order to adjust and achieve goals. They will talk openly about what needs to change and will cooperate with discussions around growth and changes, but even when they agree with the goals, their efforts will fall short of actually applying the required changes. People who DO change continuously apply change. Cooperation alone does not qualify.

APPLYING NEEDED ADJUSTMENTS

Sometimes it's very clear that people are blocking your organization from optimizing productivity and accessing its full potential. In other cases, the role people play and the resistance underlying performance problems is subtler or even invisible.

Chris's example is a great one in this sense. As the president of a startup in the high-tech industry, Chris wondered if it was his background, coming from a large established corporation, which was making his perspective so different from the perspective of others on his leadership team.

"Probably the most important thing for us right now is alignment and structure. Growing successfully beyond a startup requires aligning the functions of different departments under a clear vision. Most of our team is accustomed to responding moment by moment so we are not focused in our efforts. In my opinion we need more focus and cross-functional communications as well as structure and organization...I find before we can do that we first all need to agree this is what we need." President, high-tech industry

As a president working with extremely talented teams of engineers, Chris kept hearing teams voice a need for more clarity, more focus and most importantly more structure. This problem could easily have been tagged as a process issue, redefining structures and procedures while ignoring the importance of addressing people who don't want to change. Chris wondered why other people on the leadership team didn't see the need for structure as a priority? Why was it they were still operating in startup mode when people kept asking for more clarity? Did the leadership team not see that the fluidity of the business made it very difficult for people to be productive? These thoughts had been running through Chris's mind for over a year now, and he wondered what he could do to help support the leadership of the business move in the right direction.

While transitioning from late startup mode to a mature organizational structure, the client experienced some of the standard issues of coordinating product management and sales requirements with engineering and structural priorities. It was easy to see structures were missing. It was less obvious to see the solution was changing people who don't want to change.

Business problems are almost always associated with the way people learn, plan, interact, or execute.

Experts estimate that approximately 94% of business problems are systemic and can be attributed to the operating procedures put in place and retained by people.[7] If you look closely, you'll find the solution to almost all business problems can be assigned to adjustments people in the organization need to make.

In Chris's case, teams lacked awareness of what their own priorities were and what were the priorities of other departments. Meetings were fluid and random, and were considered a waste of time, unless they were directly linked to sales and immediate product management. Longer term and wider thinking was missing. Leaders and teams often ran into critical information in casual conversation or by accident and typically at the last moment. Many efforts were redundant, which often led to lower quality deliverables, lower customer satisfaction, and due to the high quality of people on board, lower employee satisfaction. Chris

---

7   Hans Norden, CEO EFFECTIVENESS™: *Leading a Business Beyond the Possibility of Defeat*, 17th Annual International Deming Research Seminar, New York 2011

brought the topic up for discussion several times, especially once he noticed several of his top performers were seeking employment with the organization's competition.

While decision makers often assign the solution to new procedures, values, or otherwise finding how people need to operate for the problem to go away, they often miss asking a few important questions:

→ If we haven't yet identified the solution, why are we not doing whatever needs to be done in order to identify it?

→ If we have already identified what needs to change, why have we not adopted it into practice?

→ If we don't all agree on the same solution, what are we missing that will allow us to reach an agreement, and why are we not acquiring it and integrating it into practice?

It's not so much that people in the organization lack the skills and perspectives needed in order to meet needs and achieve goals. It's the fact people don't make needed changes and adjustments in order to acquire these skills and perspectives.

If your team is missing a skill, but has the foundation to identify which skill is missing and then acquire the skill, the team would have acquired the skill already.

Giving managers the ability to change people opens a door that until now has been nailed shut. The result is people make needed adjustments, allowing organizations to optimize productivity and access the organization's full potential.

For Chris, the experience felt freeing. *"This process is absolutely brilliant. It cuts through the confusion. It allowed us to pinpoint exactly what we needed to invest in, including getting everyone to execute it consistently. We were impressed by how seamless and deliberate the solution was."* President, high-tech industry

THE IMPORTANCE OF A TEAM'S ONGOING ABILITY TO CHANGE

In most complex business situations, if the team is equipped with the right system, the team itself can reach right decisions by exploring and effectively examining different perspectives within the organization.

A team that can continuously and effectively examine what is missing, acquiring it and making needed adjustments is a team equipped to excel. It's often the case, however, that teams are missing some of the tools needed for their success. Still, they don't go about acquiring those or making needed adjustments. In these cases, teams don't independently learn and correct what's needed in order to achieve desired goals. When people don't want to change, teams don't self correct. Certain things, typically issues that lead to less-than-optimal interactions and processes in the organization, fester, build frustration, lead to loss of trust, and other crisis generating conditions.

Johan had every reason to believe his team was highly capable. The company had invested in people from its inception, and as the CEO, Johan could see the strong culture certainly paid off. It was only after the team doubled and tripled in size that the speed of change was overwhelming and needed some attention: *"We have experienced several waves of growth over the past two years. In the first year we have quadrupled in size; we are now ten times bigger than we were two years ago. With growth came new challenges."* CEO, security software industry

One new issue was team leaders were promoted to higher management positions without sufficient managerial experience. There was no time to invest in preparing them. Because of the speedy growth, a second new issue was people on the leadership team were taking on multiple functions, were overloaded, and didn't feel their efforts were optimized.

That said, there were no visible problems and the company exceeded its goals if anything. Johan was initially skeptical. He didn't really see the value of a further investment in people. He was only willing to sample the solution on one team, not because he believed in the need himself, but because of the insistence of members on his leadership team.

Frequently, teams cannot access their full potential because leaders don't see the need to change. As you'll later see, the inability to see the need for change and the inability to change are related.

While other leaders on the team were concerned about the readiness of junior management to take on more complex projects and about their own inability to keep up with the load on their desks, Johan dismissed these concerns. It's possible that if Johan's organization continued without preparing junior managers for their new roles, the company would have been extremely successful anyway. It's often the case however, that such blind areas get the best of companies, especially when several leaders in the organization have reasons to be concerned.

Of course not every objection means people objecting should be considered people who don't want to change. Sometimes people resist adopting a new system or a new solution because they believe that solution is flawed in some way. They are truly objecting for valid reasons and have nothing but the best interests of the business in mind. In those cases, it's actually important to listen and redesign the solution rather than try to force a flawed solution. Ironically, when that's the case and valuable objections are not integrated into needed solutions, someone in the organization, typically in a leadership position, needs to change.

It was only after Johan saw the difference in the performances of the single team solution that he realized which changes were needed. The block wasn't the fact that managers were not trained; it was Johan's lack of willingness to explore potential risks threatening the business.

Once the solution was implemented, including several issues Johan didn't notice before, Johan could see the value in retrospect.

"This was our first time working with a consulting company. I wanted to try this solution because, unlike other things I was offered in the past, it did not pretend to know what we needed, instead it made our team better use what we know. Now we can continue doing the many things we did right before, but the benefit is our own principles have come to the surface, and we now know how to use them deliberately, making our culture even stronger. This clarity throughout the ranks is of great benefit." CEO, security software industry

You can do so many things right, but your team's productivity can still be blocked by people who don't change. You can be the greatest CEO, strategist, project manager, change manager, or trainer. You can have excellent systems, structures, processes, and technology, but, in the end, it comes down to people. The more people in your organization get stuck in resistance, even if they themselves are not aware of it, the less successful you will be.

With constant changes in business and the need to increase people productivity, it's of great benefit to have a system that can pinpoint what a specific team needs in order to change. This book is about a system that will allow your team to acquire the skills, tools, models, and systems that will lead to desired results.

CHAPTER 1:
TAKEAWAYS

- ★ Most business challenges are in one way or another related to people not making needed adjustments.

- ★ When people do not change and adjust in a way that matches the needs and goals of the business, it's impossible for organizations to access optimal productivity.

- ★ People who don't change are not a rare few individuals, they are the majority.

- ★ The reality of the 21st century is change from technology, regulations, global competition and innovation is relentless. People are frequently experiencing forced change simply because change is imperative for the survival and success of business.

- ★ Most people, don't make desired adjustments because they don't have access to the right system for acquiring change.

- ★ There is a new way, a system that addresses these challenges head-on, equipping managers and teams with a concrete toolkit to overcome needed challenges and to directly achieve desired outcomes.

FIVE MYTHS

There are five myths that have shaped solutions in the past, making it nearly impossible to change people who don't want to change.

Influencing other people is an extremely difficult thing to do, even when people DO want to change.

Changing people requires walking a very specific path. If your team refuses to change and adjust in order to meet new needs, it's our experience that we would not be able to help you unless you facilitated them to walk on that path. It required many failures for us to identify the specific settings and conditions that are required in order to achieve 90% success.

People's belief about changing resistant people is absolutely justified. It makes sense because the right conditions were not accessed before. In the wrong conditions, the divide grows.

What leaders often don't know is that there is a gate that allows managers and leaders to enter an area that seemed inaccessible before. That gate is not yet marked and the path to it is only now being established. In fact, we have found that the path itself is very narrow. There are very specific conditions that must be maintained. Walking the path with very little deviation will mean a 90% success at changing other people even if initially they didn't want to change.

We know the path leads to the gate and the gate is there because we were able to enter it repeatedly and in a predictable way.

It's not that changing people is easy and it's even more difficult when people don't want to change. To succeed, you must be the protector of the path, making sure people don't steer off course. But once you do it, you can repeat it with consistent success 90% of the time.

There are five myths at the base of many traditional solutions. These myths are standing in your way of being a successful guardian of the path, blocking you from changing people who don't want to change and people who seem unable to change:

➜ **MYTH #1:** People often think personalities are fixed.
   FACT: As you'll see when I cover research about the brain's plasticity, the neural-synaptic pathways that are representations of most of our personality traits can be changed if people use the right system to make needed change.

➜ **MYTH #2:** Managers who try to influence other people to make needed adjustments often believe that more information and better logical information will get people to change.
   FACT: 90%-98% of people will not change in a lasting way as a result of more transparency, information or better reasoning.

➜ **MYTH #3:** Most leaders, managers, and change agents believe that in order to get people to change, people first need to trust the change agent.

FACT: Trust is a byproduct of an effective change effort and there is no need to establish it first.

➔ **MYTH #4:** Most change agents believe it's best to avoid resistance unless it is actively blocking progress.

FACT: Exposing resistance in a manageable way as early as possible reveals the inevitable under better controlled conditions, so needed changes don't drag on forever.

➔ **MYTH #5:** The history of consulting models conditioned people to believe you should hire an outside expert to be the change agent.

FACT: There are many critical reasons for managers to be the change agents.

Thanks to advanced research in different sub areas of brain science, there are now sufficient reasons to suggest the above five myths should no longer serve us in designing change solutions. Breaking these myths and developing experiences that reinforce a new reality, allows you to complete the process with much greater chances of success. Let's go over them in greater detail.

MYTH #1: PERSONALITIES ARE FIXED

What we see as challenging personalities is real. If you have tried to get difficult people and cultures to make needed changes and adjustments, you know that in some cases an individual, a team or an entire organization may be nearly impossible to change. As a result you may have mistakenly concluded that the culture or personalities are fixed, but it may have been because you didn't have access to the right toolkit.

Janet inherited her team from a previous director who managed the department for over ten years. She was hired, among other things because she believed that academic offices should be run like a profit center. As a director, she had the expectation that she would invest her time in promoting the department and in strategic issues, but instead she felt she was drawn into the nitty-gritty of production. *"My team is downright lazy. I have no better way of describing it. If I don't ask for things, no one else will think about them or initiate them. If I do ask for things I need to spend half of my time answering a million questions that could have been answered with just a small effort on their part. The personality of everyone on the team is nice, but passive. I sometimes wonder if I am the only one who really cares about the quality of our results."* Director, Engagement and Outreach, education industry

In her own words, Janet felt her team has the mentality of working in the not-for-profit world. Goals were frequently not met, people often spent their time doing tasks but without direct output that could be associated with needed outcomes. She felt everything was moving in slow motion for no reason other than some attitude that she believed was associated with the personality of the individuals on the team.

When we put personality into brain science terms, scientists now believe that who people are reflects patterns of interconnectivity of neurons and synapses in the brain. In a way, what we used to call personality is heavily influenced by a collection of patterns that we have reinforced for many years, creating a strong enough "imprint" in the way our neurons communicate.

SYNAPTIC PATHWAYS AND PEOPLE WHO DON'T WANT TO CHANGE

People are born with a system that allows them to modify the evolutionary wiring in their brain through experience. As people experience things, they start refining invisible operational rules. These are guidelines, formulated through life experiences. They are the "programming" for how people think and respond. It's an infrastructure that influences the way people learn, plan, interact and execute. It defines people's access to their potential.

Unlike any other cells in the human body, brain cells (or neurons) directly communicate with one another through synaptic connections. A synaptic pathway in the brain is a specific sequence of electric pulses. As neurons fire, the electric transmission travels through specific synapses.

An easy way to think about synaptic activity and how people respond is to imagine that each such specific sequence represents a specific conclusion or definition. If you had a bad experience with smoking for example, your brain may be triggered to have a repulsed response, represented as a specific synaptic pathway in the brain, each time you see someone smoking. In the same way, each time you hear a certain word, such as peacock, a specific sequence is initiated and so on.

The synaptic pathways that each and every member of your team uses in order to learn, plan, interact, and execute define your team's outcomes.

Neuroscientists now have solid proof that the brain's plasticity, the brain's ability to make changes to its neural-synaptic systems, doesn't stop as one ages.

A simple way to think about the way new synaptic pathways are created is to see the infrastructure of neurons and synaptic connections in the brain as a complex grid of communication channels. There are billions of specific pathways the brain can use. Who we are can be seen as a representation of the paths we end up using. The brain only rarely creates new infrastructure, but it can change the channels it is using. It's a lot like using the same route while driving your car to work every day and then deciding that from tomorrow you are going to drive through street X instead of through street Y. Street X was there all along; you simply didn't reinforce using it.

While the brain very rarely creates new communication channels as we grow older, we can start using paths that were left "dormant" before. New research in neuroplasticity shows that though the infrastructure of neural activities is set at an early age, the brain can still develop new synaptic pathways throughout people's lifetime.

Difficult people as well as most people in general are in a way trapped in patterns they have reinforced for years. Their personality is a representation of the synaptic pathways they are using, but those can be redirected under certain conditions.

We think of personality as something that cannot change, and indeed there are aspects of who we are that cannot be changed, but most of what we think is personality is actually people's inability to break patterns without the support of the right system.

What Janet identified as the personality of people on her team was people's behavioral patterns that were reinforced sufficiently in synaptic activity to be the default response. Changing those behavioral patterns depends on the ability of the solution to change synaptic pathways in the brain.

Since scientists didn't know how to establish new synaptic pathways in the past, people have come to believe that personality is fixed. It's now possible for leaders to let go of that myth.

It's of course not always wise to invest in changing people. Sometimes the investment doesn't justify the expected return. This is where quality recruiting is very helpful. When it comes to individuals, it often only makes sense to invest in change when that individual has great impact on the system as a whole, and when that individual cannot be easily replaced.

This isn't the case when whole teams or organizations are not making needed adjustments, where the costs for not changing are much higher. In some situations it certainly makes sense to hire an individual that already has more effective synaptic pathways to replace an individual that isn't a good match. A team cannot be replaced as easily, especially in knowledge-intensive industries.

Janet's team had such invisible synaptic pathways that created behavioral patterns. Since Janet couldn't see what those synaptic pathways were and since she didn't have access to a system that could replace the behavioral patterns with new, more effective ones, Janet concluded these were personality issues. Janet could see the gap between her own behavioral patterns and those of the team. In most cases, managers like Janet cannot afford to replace the team. They can however "reprogram" the team's wiring. In most cases creating new, more effective synaptic pathways as the new default response allows organizations to keep the team, with all the benefits that go with it, but literally change the people on the team at the same time.

Scientists found comprehensive ways to create new synaptic pathways only in the last decade, which is one of two reasons why the myth that personality is fixed is so strong.

The second reason is that certain changes cannot happen until certain prerequisite changes are acquired. It's often the case that people don't want to change because they don't have access to strategies that are at the foundation of making the needed adjustments.

STRATEGIES AS THE CORE OF PEOPLE'S ABILITY TO CHANGE

Strategies are the invisible operational rules the brain encodes in synaptic pathways. These are representations of how we see the world, and they directly impact how we respond to different situations.

Strategies are not skills or habits. They can be compared to lenses because they form how people see things and what they see.

In comparison to other strategies, Key Strategies are both prerequisites and more successful at achieving desired outcomes. I will discuss this in much more depth in later chapters. For now, suffice it to say that not all strategies are created equal. When people have reinforced a synaptic pathway that steers them to focus on pleasing other people, they may first need to form a new synaptic pathway that allows them to feel comfortable with other people's discomfort, before they can acquire certain sales skills, for example. Another example is people who will first need to form new synaptic pathways for systemic thinking and critical thinking before they can be innovative or apply skills around managing complex systems.

Without certain Key Strategies as a prerequisite, people will not want to change because they will not be able to change.

When managers guide people to create the needed synaptic pathways, giving people access to Key Strategies that are at the heart of the adjustments people are asked to make, personality becomes much more flexible.

What Janet perceived as personality issues were in fact people's behavioral patterns formed in response to a different management style. Janet's predecessor micromanaged the team, expecting every little detail to cross his desk before it was submitted. The team was reinforced to follow instructions and use very little independent thinking. When Janet asked them to make adjustments, they didn't understand what she was saying. The team needed a new way of seeing things in order to translate Janet's expectations into practice. *"It's unbelievable to see the transformation in the team, especially in such a short time. Suddenly, what I've been working towards for months finally got through to them. As if the light was off the entire time and now suddenly it's on. It's a transformed team and I cannot thank you enough."* Director, Engagement and Outreach, education industry

The business environment is very different than other environments, and it will take very different methods to get people to change their synaptic pathways. Managers and leaders need to guide people through the path. For that reason, it's imperative that you use a system that is clear and repeatable like the one presented later in the book.

MYTH #2: BELIEF THAT MORE INFORMATION AND BETTER LOGIC WILL CHANGE PEOPLE

Sometimes managers and change agents believe that if they could provide better explanations, reasoning, or transparency, people will be more likely to integrate the needed changes into practice.

While the above components have high correlation with people's cooperation, they are insufficient conditions. People will be more motivated by having greater ability to influence their own environment, to contribute by being more involved, and so on. Motivation will, of course, impact attitude, but as I discussed in the first chapter, attitude and even cooperation don't necessarily mean application.

Brain research in recent years explores two different

systems in the brain, one for storing knowledge and one for encoding experience.

The two systems, the Knowledge Based System (KBS) and the Experience Based System (EBS) work on different brain wavelengths and serve very different purposes.

THE ROLE OF KBS AND EBS IN CHANGING PEOPLE WHO DON'T WANT TO CHANGE

The Knowledge Based System (KBS) in the brain is designed to store and retrieve knowledge. It seeks organization, understanding, logic, coherency, consistency and accuracy. The KBS will store messages when people are exposed to information and knowledge. It will lead to conscious awareness and storage, not to behavioral change.

The Experience Based System (EBS) is designed to create new behaviors and adjust responses according to experience. Research shows that EBS is encoded in neuro-synaptic activity throughout the brain. Brain plasticity, the brain's capacity for creating new neural connections in response to experience is part of the EBS.

In general terms, every time you do something two different systems are activated in your brain: the EBS deals with the experience of what you are doing while the KBS stores the information about what you do. The experience is very different than what you know about the experience.

The Experience Based System (EBS) is designed to work as a sort of internal simulator, giving people the ability to learn nuances and adjust responses according to experience.

Some people can logically understand that one way of doing things is better than another, and then translate that understanding into the way they operate. But those people are the rare exception. Only about 2%-10% of people can, for reasons we don't yet fully understand, apply needed adjustments in practice in a lasting way as a result of new knowledge. Scientists believe this may happen as a result of a third system called Cortical Consolidation.

Brain science is only at the beginning of the journey to understand Cortical Consolidation and I'll discuss it more in Part Three. People do translate knowledge from the KBS to the EBS, probably by using Cortical Consolidation. It happens in 2%-10% of cases but it is possible. When scientists learn more about Cortical Consolidation, it's not inconceivable to assume that we would be able to equip more people to make the "translation" from one system to another. Perhaps then we will be able to equip people who learned things through logic to apply those needed adjustments to their lives.

Imagine in a few years, with this new knowledge, people will be able to sit in class and learn and then consistently apply those new conclusions to the world around them. In the meantime, science tells us that trying to achieve behavioral change through more information and better logic will result in 2%-10% of people making needed adjustments. Getting people to change by giving them more knowledge is applicable when people already know how to change themselves.

A great example for the difference between KBS and EBS can be found when you look at applying changes like developing a new culture throughout the organization.

Casey is the Executive Director of a very successful research organization in the nonprofit industry. Casey saw cultural differences as an important aspect of his organization's success on a daily basis. *"Diversity is a very important issue in our industry. Our teams are from all over the world, and we work with clients that come from very distinct cultures. This will come up in meetings, of course, but also because of the international nature of our teams."* Executive Director, nonprofit industry

Over the past five years, Casey led a culture of curiosity and passion around the organization's mission, but there was something about the interactions in the team that was getting in the way, like a sub-context to the way things were presented. He saw the impact of the differences in the way meetings were managed, in how people led and thought through projects, in small frictions and misunderstandings, and, of course, in how prepared his team was to do business development and engage clients during projects. Casey regularly found himself explaining to team members why people from certain cultures on the team were responding one way or another, but the frictions that resulted from the differences occurred despite of it.

Cultural differences exemplify how, in order to meet needs and achieve goals, people need to acquire new synaptic pathways before they can change and adjust.

Cultures, like many other aspects of personality and behavior, are reinforced for years. They become a part of us to the point we cannot recognize their influence on our assumptions and responses. Giving people access to more knowledge about the differences between cultures helps to some degree, but there is only so much our brain can apply from conscious memory. To create the needed changes, people need to learn by using EBS, not KBS.

In Casey's team, for example, people from European cultures were more direct and literal while team members from Asian cultures were more subtle and insinuated. While everyone could feel the impact of these two cultural aspects on communication and interactions, it was hard for team members to believe that they could adjust a lifelong, deeply embedded part of who they were. Just because Asian team members on Casey's team knew of the cultural differences, it didn't make the European directness seem less offensive.

Knowledge didn't make Asian insinuated communication, for example, more manageable for European team members.

It's also important to combine engaging the EBS with focusing on the Key Strategies that will allow people to make needed adjustments, instead of focusing on the behavioral patterns that need to change. If Casey asked European team members to be more subtle, the change would have taken years if the brain of these team members would not have rejected the change completely.

Many times managers and change agents focus on defining the desired result and the correcting behaviors that will lead to those desired results. While there are excellent resources that identify which behaviors will lead to desired results, there needs to be a system that answers a different question: what is needed in order for people who don't want to change or who can't sustain changing to acquire the above behaviors and apply them in a lasting way? In other words, it's the difference between training a sales team on better listening skills or equipping sales teams with whatever it is they need in order to acquire better listening skills.

"It was a real pleasure to work through this process. Not only did our teams develop skills that will last them a lifetime, but our managers have learned how to guide employees to adopt new needed skills. It has been without a doubt, an eye opening experience for everyone involved and we won't hesitate to use this program again in the future." Executive Director, nonprofit industry

While scientists don't know enough about turning knowledge into behavioral change, they do know enough about communicating with the EBS directly.

Instead of using the knowledge system-cortical consolidation route, you can change people by directly engaging their EBS.

The results of using the EBS are not new but unfortunately they were not accessible to business before. The Air Force has been using it for many years, training pilots by using simulators, directly reinforcing EBS. In the last ten years language teaching models have shifted from the traditional knowledge based teaching to experience based teaching, expediting the acquisition of language dramatically. Physiotherapists and physicians have had great breakthroughs by engaging EBS.

The system presented in this book would not have been possible if it wasn't for scientific developments. It's only thanks to research in brain science that we now know how to directly engage EBS and can design inexpensive and effective systems to create change where it was blocked or too slow before.

Granted, you can't change everything about people. On top of that, not everything about who we are comes from synaptic activity. There are genetic and other influences as well. Knowing the boundaries of the systems you are using is very important. But within those boundaries there is still a lot more you CAN do.

MYTH #3: FOR PEOPLE TO CHANGE THEY FIRST NEED TO TRUST THE CHANGE AGENT

Traditional change efforts will often guide organizations to first build a culture of trust as a platform for growth and for the success of future initiatives.

When trust already exists in teams, it's indeed a valuable platform. When trust doesn't exist, the first stage shouldn't be building trust, it should be getting people to acquire the Key Strategies that will change the way people resist and react.

Trust will come if the right strategies are put in place and if the experience of getting people to acquire those strategies justifies trust.

Put differently, you can achieve desired outcomes without initial trust, even if you force change. If both the team and the organization end up benefiting from the acquisition of Key Strategies and the process of the acquisition justify trust, you'll still get desired outcomes and trust will be a natural byproduct. If trust isn't there at first, you won't get to lasting trust or to desired outcomes without the right Key Strategies in place.

As you'll see in Part Two, in some cases trying to build trust first will actually make it impossible to reach desired outcomes, especially with highly manipulative teams. Furthermore, when I go over the system itself in Part Three, you'll see that people need to resist in order to acquire new strategies that contradict with their existing synaptic pathways. You'll see that if you try to build trust before aggravating resistance you will be risking dragging invisible resistance along with you, undermining genuine cooperation. Generally speaking, according to new research, the concept of building trust as a foundation for change needs to be refined and examined.

Martin was struggling to help Barbara increase the productivity of her team. As the CTO of a large semiconductor corporation, Barbara was described as controlling and as a micromanager. Her team's productivity was suffering as a result. Team members were not proactive, nor did they offer solutions to problems or initiate any growth. From his position as Senior VP of Global HR, Martin tried to support Barbara in the past, with little success.

"Barbara uses a control and divide approach. Her teams work in business and function silos, she exhibits arrogant or dominant behavior, she promotes team members that will follow her at the cost of tolerating poor performance and she often seems more concerned with personal ownership of goals at the expense of common target outcomes." Senior VP of Global HR, semiconductor industry

Trying to first establish trust with an executive like Barbara is often counterproductive. If you have ever tried to get someone like Barbara to change you may have noticed that the more you try to be respectful and prove you are worthy of their trust, the more controlling they become and the less ability you have to guide them to change.

Barbara was missing certain very specific Key Strategies and without those strategies in place, there probably was nothing Martin could say or do to get Barbara to change. In fact, trying to get Barbara to first trust Martin only made things worse. Barbara's brain was programmed to reinforce ineffective synaptic pathways or strategies to achieve control. Without the right strategies in place, Barbara continued manipulating Martin's trust building efforts, keeping with her filter of existing synaptic pathways.

The more important point isn't to build trust as a goal, it's the acquisition of needed strategies that will lead to changes in behavioral patterns. If there was a way for Barbara to acquire more effective strategies, Barbara and her team would have been able to achieve higher productivity even if Barbara or her team didn't trust Martin or each other first. Trust would have or would not have been established based on the way Barbara and her team were led through the acquisition process of the new Key Strategy.

Trust is best built as part of getting people to acquire needed Key Strategies. It's built based on the way people are led through the acquisition process. Trust does not need to come first.

It would be hard to say that Barbara's team completely trusted Barbara's new behavioral patterns would last. It would be completely wrong to suggest that Barbara trusted Martin or that the change process would serve her well when she started. But Barbara and her team were able to achieve lasting desired outcomes without initially establishing trust.

"The transformation in Barbara and more importantly in the response of Barbara's team is noticeable. Barbara is now leading a team that engages in cross functional collaboration and team work where collaborative contributions are encouraged and decisions are based on facts and merit...I don't recommend solutions lightly but this process not only proved to develop Barbara, it got her team to change in response." Senior VP of Global HR, semiconductor industry

Most people lack Key Strategies that will allow them to accept change rather than resist. Without those strategies people will always resist at the onset of the change effort, and with some it will be a tremendous waste of your time to try and establish trust first.

MYTH #4: IT'S BEST TO AVOID RESISTANCE UNLESS IT IS ACTIVELY BLOCKING PROGRESS

Managers and change agents are taught to ignore resistance, hoping that if they move forward without addressing it, they could better achieve goals. Unless resistance is actively and bluntly getting in the way of progress, we typically continue to set goals and state expectations in the belief that people who are cooperative will apply the needed changes.

As you'll see when I cover five common types of teams who don't want to change in Part Two, some types will seem cooperative, but since resistance is there, they will not make needed adjustments or make required changes.

Resistance isn't an attitude and it isn't a spirit of cooperation. It's only measured by lack of application.

Over the years we have noticed that when people try to change, resistance is triggered at a very specific stage, reaching its peak at a very specific moment (to learn more about the scientific explanation of resistance go to Research on www.

KeyChangeNow.com). We have found that orchestrating the appearance of resistance and how to exit it quickly is one of the most important components for people's ability to acquire needed strategies.

Resistance itself is a representation of the strategies people are missing. If people are missing the strategy that allows them to gain control effectively, they will resist by trying ineffectively to gain control. Resistance comes in different shades and colors. The specific resistance teams exhibit will be colored by the strategies that team is missing.

The solution for overcoming resistance isn't to ignore it. The best way to deal with resistance is to equip teams with the strategies that will remove resistance from its core. It's a solution that combines Key Strategies with a five-stage acquisition system. It takes combining both aspects to make it possible for you to achieve high success rates and you'll find a more detailed explanation of the acquisition system itself in Part Three.

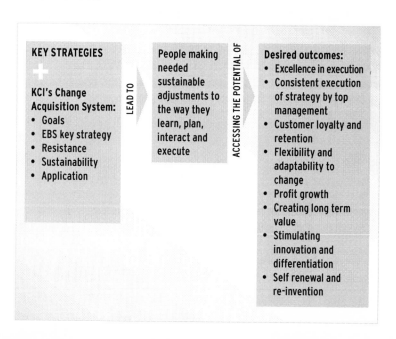

We spent over 10 years refining what makes Key Strategies stronger and how people can acquire those new strategies quickly to achieve desired outcomes. Until we get to the acquisition system itself, the most important thing to notice at this point is that when people need to acquire new Key Strategies that contradict with existing strategies, it's natural, needed, and predictable for people to resist before they can sustain a new strategy.

Addressing resistance sooner rather than later offers you a way to accelerate change. To achieve desired outcomes, you need to address the inevitable as soon as possible, under your own conditions and with specific techniques.

MYTH #5: YOU CAN HIRE AN OUTSIDE EXPERT TO BE THE CHANGE AGENT

John, a Deputy Director General in a small hospital, found the productivity of Lisa's team concerning. It was draining his time and energy. Lisa was responsible for a team who provided many valuable services to the hospital's doctors and patients. John believed the team wasn't made up of the right individuals and roles were probably not defined well enough.

"The girls respect Lisa however they argue and don't cooperate with each other and with her. There is frequently some kind of drama going on. This naturally affects performances. Doctors get less than par service. At times, the girls will argue while doctors or clients are present. Lisa is a great professional. Her difficulty is with receiving feedback. Anytime I try to give her feedback about how she is running the team, I feel like she isn't listening. She'll either quickly agree with me or say she already knows the problem. She gets defensive." Deputy Director General, medical industry

John's initial preference was to send the team to an offsite workshop to work through the issues and find solutions. He was frustrated with Lisa's performances and, due to past interactions with her, he didn't believe she could lead this transformation. He certainly saw Lisa as part of the problem, but he didn't necessarily see her as part of the solution.

When you need to change people, it's not the best time to hire outside change agents. The best position to lead teams out of resistance is the position that has the authority to hold the team accountable and support the team in overcoming resistance. Experts can support managers, but for many reasons it's better to equip managers to guide people who don't want to change through the process.

Organizational development originally shared many themes with medical paradigms. The idea that an expert, doctor, therapist or consultant would identify what's wrong and tell you how to fix it was at the foundation of many models. The doctor or the consultant was not only the diagnostician but was also the change agent. With the development of other sciences, and especially brain science, this model is gradually being replaced. In the new model, experts educate clients about the decisions they have to make.

While the main emphasis of the medical model used to be the knowledge and accuracy of the doctor or the expert, the emphasis of the system in this book is acquisition and effective application. Instead of focusing on the knowledge and perspective that experts can give, the focus shifts to designing processes that measure what the client "gets" and applies. In the medical profession, the diagnosis is now becoming gradually second to making sure the patient applies the right life choices.

With this new emphasis, the question "What is the problem and what should be done to solve it?" becomes secondary to a different set of questions. "What should be different in order for the team to solve the problem on its own?" and "What is required for the team to apply needed adjustments?" are now more important than the conclusions experts can offer.

Solutions no longer prioritize knowing what's wrong over change. New solutions prioritize knowing every detail of what's wrong at a far second to designing solutions that lead to integration, application, and execution.

Managers must be an integral part of leading change for it to be applied in a lasting way.

In order to change in a way that will optimize productivity and give your organization access to its fullest potential, you must make sure that managers are aligned with the effort you are making. It's only then that changes can be achieved and sustained.

It's further important that managers lead the process and not just participate in it as part of the team. The assumption we are making is that, in some cases if the manager and the organization as a whole had the toolkit to manage the dynamics of the team effectively, the problem wouldn't have existed in the first place. It follows logic then to make sure managers and the organization are both equipped with that very toolkit.

The main consideration should always be that when the expert leaves, effective practices have already been applied, so that the manager will be prepared and equipped to continue with very minimal external support, if any. Having the manager participate as part of the team is like teaching someone to drive by having them watch an expert drive. It's only when the manager starts driving that you'll see what he or she still needs in order to drive effectively. This real practice should start as soon as possible.

By learning how to guide her team through the five-stage process I discuss in Part Three, Lisa was able to refine her own Key Strategies, become more open and attentive in her responses to feedback, and position herself effectively as the leader of the team.

"The skill of this process is seen in the ability to cut to the

chase and discern critical problems within an organization. The clarity it brings to bear is astounding. Furthermore, the solutions are practical, easily implemented, with results easily tracked by metrics the process helps you define. Under the guidance of this process, Human Resources regained the meaning of treating people as powerful resources within my organization, and not just frustrating pawns in a very difficult chess game." Deputy Director General, medical industry

Equipping managers to be change agents often allows for additional information to surface about the organization as a whole. At times, the forces blocking the team are tied to the organization's culture, the dynamics between the manager and other managers, or the structure of the organization which are defined by senior leadership.

Organizations then may or may not decide to address issues that have a wider effect on the organization, but the importance of this is that it gives the process the right foundation needed in order to save resources. Targeting the right issue not only saves time and money, it also assures that the organization will be able to prevent other issues and solve most of the problems on its own, without the need for additional external support. It means that, as a result of the process, the organization has directly increased its ability to optimize its productivity, gaining access to its full potential.

CHAPTER 2:
TAKEAWAYS

★ Resistance isn't an attitude and it isn't a spirit of cooperation. It's a lack of application.

★ Most of what we think is personality and cannot be changed is actually people's inability to break patterns without external support.

★ Without certain Key Strategies as a prerequisite, people will not want to change because they will not be able to change.

★ Only about 2%-10% of people can, for reasons we do not yet fully understand, apply needed adjustments in practice in a lasting way as a result of new knowledge. Scientists believe this may happen as a result of the involvement of a third system called Cortical Consolidation.

★ Instead of using the knowledge system-cortical consolidation route, you can change people by directly engaging their EBS.

★ Trust is best built as part of getting people to acquire needed Key Strategies. It's built based on the way people are led through the acquisition process. Trust doesn't need to come first.

★ Resistance comes in different shades and colors. The specific resistance teams exhibit will be colored by the strategies that team is missing.

★ The best position to lead teams to exit resistance is the position that has the authority to hold the team accountable.

PART TWO
5 TEAMS WHO DON'T WANT TO CHANGE

People are programmed to interact with their environment according to very specific rules they have established through experience. These rules, or strategies as we call them, can be either extremely effective, giving individuals, teams, and organizations access to optimal productivity, or they can get in the way.

When certain specific combinations of strategies are missing they increase the likelihood for certain behaviors, team dynamics, leadership styles, business outcomes, and resistance responses. Five such combinations or clusters of missing strategies and the outcomes associated with them are introduced in Part Two:

→ Doubtful analyst teams
→ Emotional oscillator teams
→ Pleasing teams
→ Flamboyant teams
→ Stability teams

A team will be considered to need a certain cluster of strategies, not because all of the individuals on the team are lacking the same strategies, but because the interaction and dynamic in the team is consistently lacking the application of those needed strategies.

The strategies teams need to focus on will target the core solution and will allow the team to optimize productivity, maximize the team's strengths and minimize the team's weaknesses.

You are learning about these clusters in Part Two so that you will be able to utilize the acquisition system presented in Part Three to change these clusters.

Part Two will give you the context of the specific responses each cluster exhibits, how each cluster thinks, reacts and resists. Part Three will then allow you to reference how a single acquisition system applies.

In order to give teams the gift of being more adaptive, cooperative and resourceful, you need to equip them with specific Key Strategies. To do that we:

1. Pinpoint which Key Strategies are needed in order for the team to make needed adjustments in a lasting way using a unique assessment process

2. Equip you to guard the path of changing people who don't want to change so that resistance is exposed and managed quickly and seamlessly.

3. Help you guide teams to lasting application and execution of needed adjustments, accelerating the acquisition of Key Strategies by following a five-stage acquisition system that we will explore in Part Three.

DOUBTFUL ANALYST TEAMS

"If I disagree, it means you are wrong."

When a Key Strategy is missing, it leaves traces in everything people do, from the way they interact to the way they make decisions and the way they execute tasks. People who are lacking the needed synaptic pathways to notice details, for example, will lack attention to detail in writing, presenting, and listening. It will be to different degrees at different times but it will be there.

Doubtful analyst teams need very specific Key Strategies in order to optimize productivity and access their full potential.

Andrew's meeting with Eric went better than Andrew hoped. Andrew's team had a somewhat traditional title under customer care, but there was nothing traditional about the project they were heading. Andrew led a cultural transformation effort, and since Eric was the VP of technology, Andrew hoped Eric would influence his team to cooperate with Andrew's team. *"Customer care is still interpreted differ-*

ently by each and every person you talk to, but I strongly believe it holds the key for our success, not just in sales but in innovation and market leadership. The challenge is to create measurable success that can be associated with customer care. We have a great team, resources and the support of our CEO but the biggest challenge remains dissemination, integrating this new approach on the cellular level, getting to every last employee..." Director of Customer Care, security software industry

To increase adoption of the new culture, Andrew and his team collected case studies and success stories from clients highlighting the influence quality customer care had on customer loyalty and sales. Though Andrew had the support of the organization's leadership team, he didn't see much progress integrating the new approach. He chose to start the campaign in the sales team. He suspected the effort wasn't successful there because the VP of sales was under too much pressure. Andrew hoped the first breakthrough could be achieved with another department.

Doubtful analyst teams are highly skeptical, generally dismissive and tend to disagreement. Typically disagreements in these teams are not discussed and are followed by lack of application around anything they see differently.

When Andrew's team met with IT, it didn't help that Andrew tried to establish the importance of customer care. The team responded with glazed-over looks and dismissal. People in the IT team could not see why customer care would have anything to do with them. Prioritizing customer care above functionality and technical design within development specifications didn't make sense to the team in the same way it made sense to Andrew. IT deals with technology, not people! It was clear to Andrew that if they didn't agree and see things eye to eye, the new culture wouldn't be implemented here either.

It's relatively easy to identify doubtful analyst teams by their declared values, high standards and principles, strong personal convictions, and intense sense of right and wrong. They follow clear internal standards rich in "shoulds" and "musts" and they expect others to follow those same standards as well. Communication in these teams is often formed as arguments in which people are trying to convince each other they are right. Teams and individuals that belong to this cluster are reliable, respectful, extremely loyal, hard workers and typically ambitious. The expectation in the team will be to have rational and emotionally detached dynamics, making sure team members' own wants and needs are minimized by self discipline. You will see these teams trying to control their environment with orderliness and often cleanliness, both in thinking and in their actual physical environment. When other teams don't meet the same standards as the doubtful analyst's standards, they will complain and expect others to change. This often means doubtful analyst teams will not make adjustments to cooperate with others who work differently than they do.

This kind of team is suspicious, and since they try to control emotional expressions, will not appreciate being told by others how they feel or what their dynamic reveals. They will often dispute any suggestion that you know something about them that they don't know, or that they could possibly be blind to something they are involved in. They don't like extreme statements or exaggerations and they may be very suspicious of statements made by other team members.

Without certain prerequisite strategies, teams cannot make the changes you need them to make.

People in these teams believe they know where things should be and how to fix things that are not where they should be. These teams filter and judge everything that is being said to them, and unless something makes sense to them they will not cooperate. It's faulty to think that using their language and trying to communicate with them through logic, or providing them with more information, will get them to agree and hence to make needed adjustments. As you'll later see, our experience shows this approach frequently doesn't work with doubtful analyst teams. It will often lead to long debates about little things followed by little progress. This makes decision making in these teams very difficult and often one sided, at times creating lack of coordination, redundancy and contradicting efforts.

Doubtful analyst teams are rigid, treating others in the team or outside the team who have different perspectives with superiority. It's not unusual for doubtful analyst teams to treat their clients this way too, without realizing it and typically being unwilling to admit it.

Perfection is very important in these teams so they don't do well with feedback or critiques, but they constantly criticize everything, thinking it's their duty to highlight any areas of improvement. Naturally this negative atmosphere creates an environment in which new ideas or needs for improvement are not brought up for discussion. There are typically many disagreements in the team that are constantly slowing the team down. These teams often procrastinate, have time management issues due to their need to perfect things, and have a hard time starting new things because they feel everything must be done just right before it's put into action. Doubtful analyst teams will typically invest greatly in trying to avoid mistakes and this results in reduced productivity, reduced innovation, and missed opportunities.

Doubtful analyst teams need very specific strategies in order to access the team's potential.

To identify which specific strategies are needed we use a comprehensive Solution Assessment™. The assessment does not focus on which existing strategies don't serve the team well, instead it only focuses on the strategies, that if put in place, will give the team access to the team's full potential.

In Andrew's case, the assessment identified a combination of needed strategies we run into often. We see this type of team frequently, especially among engineers, scientists and people with technological expertise. The goal of the process is to put in place the needed strategies so that the IT team will be able to see things from the same systemic perspective that Andrew used.

We begin the process with clients with an assessment, identifying which strategies will lead to desired outcomes by looking at the patterns in the team and the team's environment. Unlike other assessments, the assessment we use is not descriptive. It does not present us with an outline of what is. The assessment needed in order to guide teams to desired outcomes provides us with the keys to the solution. Instead of what is, the assessment report describes what is needed.

A team is considered a doubtful analyst team not because all individuals on the team are doubtful analysts, but because of the interaction and dynamic in the team.

When our team assessment report highlights that certain Key Strategies are needed in order for the team to achieve desired outcomes, it doesn't necessarily mean that everyone on the team is missing the exact same strategies to the exact same degree.

It does mean, in practice, those Key Strategies are not being applied by the team as a whole. It means that while individual people may have different profiles, the team as a whole is not practicing a certain strategy that would allow the team to access its full potential. It's often the case that some team members have practiced the strategies the team needs as a whole in the past, but they are not bringing those effective strategies to the team because of the dynamics in the team. The dynamics can be influenced by formal or informal authority figures on the team. The proof is always in the making. If a team allows for doubtful analyst patterns to be the dominant patterns, the team will be considered a doubtful analyst team.

Providing the team as a whole with beneficial strategies allows for those effective strategies to be established where they were missing and to come to the surface where they already existed.

A new Key Strategy is not a form of convincing or directing, it's an eye opener, a new way of evaluating decisions and responses.

Acquiring a new strategy is similar to standing in a place you've never been, seeing things with completely new eyes. Once the IT team could use the new strategies, hearing Andrew's perspective and seeing its merits and applications turned into an exciting and innovative way of looking at IT.

The IT team was made up of highly intelligent individuals that used analysis almost exclusively. The mindset of analysis is one of rejection, criticism and elimination. To them being open to an idea they disagree with was a dead end. Unless the IT team could see Andrew's point of view, Andrew knew they would not cooperate with him. In this particular case, their perspective didn't match with Andrew's perspective so a deeper change was needed. In order to access their full potential, the IT team first needed to acquire a new cluster of strategies.

Once the strategies were acquired, there was no need to convince, pressure or force the new approach on the IT team. They saw what Andrew saw and were able to draw conclusions themselves. The change didn't come because Andrew's point of view made more sense. It came because the IT team was open to hearing other perspectives; open to accepting logic other than their own.

"The process put our vision to practice. Getting the IT team to open up was a lot like turning on a light switch. My team was already familiar with resistance to customer care as a new culture...we didn't realize how important it was to overcome the resistance that came from fundamentally seeing things differently. It was as if until that point we were talking two very different languages and suddenly words that before didn't make sense were finally clear." Director of Customer Care, security software industry

THE STRATEGIES NEEDED TO SUPPORT THE DOUBTFUL ANALYST TEAM

Ellen believed that in her organization, a leading semiconductor corporation, "soft skills" were equally important to all managers in the organization. *"We have two career development paths, a management path and professional path. More often than not, the nature of project work puts professionals in informal management positions. I'd like to see programs that give a better answer to professionals managing people. These experts know their work better than anyone in the company...the way they interact with people could use improvement."* VP of HR, semiconductor industry

After over 20 years in the HR profession, including 12 in senior executive positions, Ellen was confident many of the strategic issues could be resolved by addressing the leadership practices of middle management. Her message to the CEO has been the same for the last two years: "If we want to increase productivity, we need to teach managers how to facilitate and supervise teams."

When doubtful analysts are promoted to management positions they often lack people management skills, and it's very difficult to get them to acquire new, more effective behaviors around interaction and communication.

Three Key Strategies have the highest correlation with the doubtful analyst team. The relevance of the strategies is determined not only by the profile of the team, but by the specific desired outcomes defined for the team. When the right strategies are acquired, resistance drops, doubtful analysts gain access to skills they could not apply before and the change is lasting. The key to success is consistent indications of change in application. These developments should be identified by the team who needs to change, but more importantly by the leaders who initiated the change, and by other teams and colleagues independently interacting with the team.

The following Key Strategies allow doubtful analyst teams to optimize productivity, giving them access to their potential:

→ Synthesis vs. Analysis
→ Multiple Truths
→ Dynamic Hierarchy of Values

STRATEGY #1: SYNTHESIS VS. ANALYSIS

Most people are more comfortable using either synthesis or analysis as their primary way of thinking. This Key Strategy creates a new way of looking at the world. Instead of letting what people are accustomed to dictate their response, Synthesis vs. Analysis plants the ability to distinguish which situation requires analysis and which requires synthesis. With this new strategy, the type of thinking is selected by the requirements of the task rather than by an autopilot response.

Doubtful analyst teams have a strong preference for analysis and will only use synthesis for a limited number of tasks. Expanding their use of synthesis in the right contexts makes them generally more flexible, open, inclusive, and caring.

This strategy gives doubtful analyst teams access to a more open, intuitive, systemic view when it comes to interacting with people, solving complex dynamic problems, responding quickly to a changing environment, quickly making complex decisions, having more tolerance for ambiguity and more.

Though analysis is the preferred approach for the doubtful analyst, these teams are often highly intelligent with good mastery of both analysis and synthesis. It's not that they need to learn about synthesis. It's that they need to reinforce when to use it effectively.

The managers that needed this strategy in the above leading semiconductor corporation had a clear preference for analysis and didn't use Synthesis vs. Analysis selectively. As a result, these managers were blocked from accessing their potential in discussions, interactions and communication. They could not acquire new skills and habits around communication for example, before acquiring this first strategy because in this case Synthesis vs. Analysis was a prerequisite strategy.

STRATEGY #2: MULTIPLE TRUTHS

This Key Strategy is the ability to allow contradicting truths to co-exist. It's an openness to admit not seeing everything or seeing things incorrectly. Doubtful analyst teams think in polarized terms: if one option is right other options must be wrong, if someone is going to win, then someone else must lose. They typically believe they know what is right and what is wrong.

Without this Key Strategy, doubtful analysts that are promoted to management positions are too directive and controlling. They often miss what other people mean and typically don't notice cues unless someone tells them what's going on literally. They can get very frustrated because they often think that other people's insistence isn't justified, and that others don't understand when it's them who are not hearing what others are saying. They come across disinterested, impatient, judgmental, and often condescending. In team settings, the lack of this strategy prevents effective communication, reduces the effectiveness of planning, gets in the way of seeing the whole picture and makes conflicts last forever.

Most importantly, for doubtful analyst teams, this strategy impacts their communication style. They start understanding that different points of view can co-exist and can develop more effective listening and discussion skills.

STRATEGY #3: DYNAMIC HIERARCHY OF VALUES

Sometimes, values and rules that work in certain situations don't apply in other situations. This strategy is an ability to flexibly evaluate, on an ongoing basis, the way people's goals or values are defined in respect to needs in reality. It means people's internal, preconceived rules are not above reality and that people trust themselves to negotiate the rules in perspective to new situations.

Doubtful analyst teams are typically very rigid, which often leads to unnecessary, less than effective responses, as well as missing clues and opportunities that are right under their noses. This often gets in the way of effective prioritization.

Acquiring this Key Strategy creates a new way for doubtful analyst teams to look at the world. Instead of a rigid definition of how things always are, doubtful analyst teams start adjusting to different situations with greater flexibility. They learn to accept there's more than one way to approach things successfully. As they leave their preconceived perceptions behind, these teams often start noticing many more opportunities and options, becoming extremely innovative, creative and effective.

Ellen felt that working with middle management has made a big difference to productivity and morale. The process allowed her to tap into the great talent that the organization's professional channel had to offer. The managers who acquired the strategies were top achievers in their previous roles and now Ellen believed most of them were prepared to be top achievers in more senior positions.

"Seeing the transformation in managers was incredible, especially since the training was done virtually. The managers who went through the program were very satisfied, but most importantly, the transformation was experienced by the teams themselves." VP of HR, semiconductor industry

It's important to note that people behave differently under different circumstances, when they are around different people and especially when they are forced to change.

When you meet a doubtful analyst team for the first time, you may be presented with behaviors very different than the above description. Doubtful analyst teams are charming, very genuine and impressive with their brilliant minds and level-headedness. They are kind, and since they think of themselves as very decent and fair, they will often present quite a balanced perspective. This charming state is the way these teams operate when there's no conflict or discomfort.

Teams that belong to this cluster will be in this state for as long as they feel appreciated. They are generally brilliant and tolerant enough so they mostly adjust to external change relatively well. It's when they are asked to adjust how they operate or make changes to decisions they believe in that the doubtful analyst will adopt their other characteristics. If you withdraw the need for them to adjust or change, they will typically return to their original charming state.

While the five clusters presented in this book are very distinct, they can also be deceptive.

This is important because misidentifying needed Key Strategies will not lead to desired outcomes. If the wrong strategies are acquired in a lasting way, they will not allow the team to achieve desired outcomes. This is where an expert assessment is truly invaluable.

THE DOUBTFUL ANALYST TEAM BLOCKING DESIRED RESULTS

Though results vary in different industries and countries, studies show that certain challenges are ranked highest in importance among CEOs. The top challenges include:

→ Excellence in execution
→ Consistent execution of strategy by top management
→ Customer loyalty and retention
→ Speed, flexibility and adaptability to change

Helping organizations change people who don't want to change isn't only about changing behavior. It's about giving people the platform they need in order to make the adjustments that will in turn lead to desired outcomes. Without Key Strategies, 90% of people will not want to change, often as a result of not being able to change.

Doubtful analyst teams often block organizations from achieving excellence in execution because they tend to think they are right, preventing processing of input from others and delaying needed results and quality of service.

Rachael led the cultural change in her organization. With over ten years in strategic HR positions in the IT industry, seven of which with her current employer, Rachael could almost predict the response she would get from different managers. *"We are going through this transformation so that our corporate culture will be aligned with the demands of the 21st century. It will be a strategic advantage if everyone in the organization communicated with the same values. If we live by those values they will project to our interactions with clients."* VP of HR, IT industry

It seemed like some teams would be more likely to accept certain values and that some would be more open to change in general. The team that Rachael wanted to pay extra attention to was the systems team. Historically this team was less open to workshops, training or development work, and Rachael was concerned this time would be no different.

The cultural change would address agility, an extremely hard aspect for the systems team. The goal was for the team to minimize monitoring efforts, avoid "paralysis by analysis" or being overly rigid about processes and diverse needs. It seemed the transformation would be hardest in the systems team because this team would overact at any slight mid-course correction, they often delayed for too long before making movement generating decisions and they focused excessively on minor differences and internal issues.

Rachael and the leadership of the organization had already done extensive work defining what they wanted to achieve. The main support they wanted was to get people in the systems team to make needed adjustments, translating new values into daily ongoing practices.

Without the three strategies, Synthesis vs. Analysis, Multiple Truths, and a Dynamic Hierarchy of Values, the systems team could not adopt the new values. Asking people on a doubtful analyst team to be inclusive or flexible without first equipping them with the needed strategies is like asking someone to read a sentence written in black ink in a pitch dark room. To see the writing, they will first need to turn on the light.

For the systems team, once the strategies were in place it was as if the lights were suddenly turned on. Until that moment, the team resisted in every way it knew how but their manager was equipped to guide them through their resistance, continuously getting them to acquire the needed strategies along the way.

"The experience was eye opening. The systems department

started from being completely internally focused, overloading the conversation with information and details but then there was a clear shift. They completed the process with most values implemented. Everyone on the team was affected starting with senior managers, all the way to team leaders and team members. The process bridged the invisible gap between strategy and execution." VP of HR, IT industry

Without needed Key Strategies, doubtful analyst teams will run projects with excellent organization and clarity, typically with a systemic understanding of the issues, but the team will move slower and with less flexibility. This affects not only team dynamics and lacking the needed sensitivity with clients, but also the ability to integrate new systems.

When the doubtful analyst cluster is the predominant cluster in leadership positions in your organization, this rigidity will also lead to lost opportunities and to risks that are associated with things taking too long. The doubtful analyst cluster will often not recognize the needs of others. Instead, people needing this cluster of strategies will try to force others to see things as they do.

Increasing the productivity of the doubtful analyst team depends not only on equipping people with the needed strategies, but also on getting those strategies to stick. This requires guiding teams through a five-stage process which I will cover in Part Three, but for now let's focus on the third stage of that process: the predictable and necessary resistance stage.

As you'll later see with other Key Strategy clusters, resistance can delay forever unless it's triggered correctly. This is important because, without overcoming resistance, 90% of people will not acquire needed strategies in a lasting way.

Teams who need certain Key Strategies, such as the pleasing team, who I will discuss in a later chapter, will initially try to avoid actively resisting in any way possible.

This is not the case here. Typically doubtful analyst teams don't need great encouragement in order to enter resistance or express resistance. These teams are typically highly suspicious, distrustful, almost constantly looking for flaws, imperfections and why things probably won't work. More than anything these teams don't like others overruling what they believe is the right answer. Since they believe they are right, if you are asking them to change, it must mean you are wrong. Since they cannot cooperate with wrong, resistance in doubtful analyst teams will come up relatively quickly and almost with no need to deliberately aggravate it.

GUIDING DOUBTFUL ANALYST TEAMS TO EXIT RESISTANCE

Over the years, working with different teams in a variety of industries, we have seen very consistent patterns around resistance. We have found teams resist according to the strategies they are missing. Different combinations of needed strategies will produce different resistance behaviors and will require different emphasis in order to guide teams to exit resistance. Once Key Strategies are in place, however, resistance patterns change. In a way, resistance can be defined as a representation of missing strategies.

When people are lacking certain strategies, everything about their decisions, behaviors, feelings, and thoughts are colored by the lack of these strategies.

In order to change how people resist, people must first acquire the strategies that will affect the way they resist. It's only after they acquire the needed strategies, that teams will change how they resist. For that initial acquisition process, teams will resist according to their profile. Until those needed strategies are in place, it's important to create the proper nuanced setting to overcome initial resistance in order to achieve the best results.

Because they believe they are right, this cluster will resist following instructions. It may take a few rounds before you'll see resistance, but when it comes, it will typically be in the form of skipped over details or a full blown challenge to the validity and usefulness of the exercise. Of all the combinations of needed strategies in this book, doubtful analyst teams are most likely to decide they don't want to cooperate.

When people don't cooperate, it does not by any means indicate you cannot successfully support these people to change. Initial motivation or engagement helps, but our success and expertise lies in the cases in which people don't want to change. The five examples presented in this book certainly include some of the extreme cases because we want you to see, that even in these cases, you can have 90% success getting people to make needed adjustments in a lasting way. Teams that will initially resist will end up changing 90% of the time.

As the COO of a medium sized biotech company, Chase was surrounded by highly analytical people. Chase himself felt very comfortable with a direct, coherent and organized way of communicating. From time to time someone would approach him with feedback and this wasn't the first time he heard things about Stephan's management style. Chase felt Stephan was a phenomenal leader. He could see the points others and especially Stephan's team made. He could see why others would think Stephan used a dismissive tone, but Stephan was one of the most brilliant team leaders Chase met and he wasn't about to lose him for the occasional incident.

"Stephan and I talked about this in the past. He knows this is how other people perceive him but that's just who he is.

Recently our HR Director brought it to my attention that several of his team members have asked to be transferred, and that's more concerning. He's brilliant, but he just doesn't work well in a team." COO, biotech industry

It seemed there have been several attempts in the past to reach out to Stephan and get him to change his behavior. He met any slight insinuation that he needed to improve with an offensive response. He often took on a defensive position, minimizing the claims others brought up by saying things like: "I was only trying to make myself clear" or deferring his response to someone else doing something wrong. Stephan often responded to requests as criticism, replied with borderline arrogance and drew on his vast knowledge base for reaffirming his opinions and dismissing other people. If asked to do something he didn't agree with, Stephan insistently asked many questions, saying he wanted to better understand, but this sent a gentle underlying message that he does not agree.

The most important key to guiding doubtful analyst teams to change is to understand what is missing for these teams and how it affects the way people think and feel. If you aim to increase the productivity of this team, it's better to avoid almost all strategies that would work for other clusters.

You don't want to gently explain or persuade doubtful analyst teams to understand your point of view. An effective definition of goals in working with Stephan included multiple perspectives, tending to his needs as well as the needs of the organization, and setting clear unwavering expectations.

If you talk to doubtful analyst teams gently about the need to develop their own abilities, they will most likely dismiss you. If you use descriptive terms about what needs to improve, they will feel threatened, interpreting your objective, logical perspective as an attempt to blame them, responding as if they are being attacked. If you express emotions or lose your balance, they will most likely see you as incoherent and therefore wrong. That is actually more dangerous because doubtful analyst teams often shut down, reducing interactions, hiding their thoughts and looking for ways out that are far from optimizing productivity. Rather, their coping methods are damaging to everyone and everything they touch.

The way doubtful analyst teams interact can trigger frustration in managers, so it's very important to prepare managers to respond to this team effectively. The know-it-all, superiority approach of this team makes some managers back off when this team starts arguing with a defensive attack-like response. In other cases, doubtful analyst teams will respond with subdued anger. Other managers may want to take control and be more forceful with these teams. Emotionality, including control related actions, that are sudden and unexplainable are considered a flaw by these teams. On the other end, any attempt to appease the doubtful analyst is very likely to be taken literally as agreement with their point of view.

It's important to avoid arguing, staying assertive and very clear about expectations and intentions and leave it at that.

The best, and perhaps the only way, we have found that consistently works, is to put their development in the hands of another doubtful analyst that they respect and defer to, making sure this manager, facilitating their development, is in agreement with the steps that need to be taken. The doubtful analyst is very sensitive to structure and proper order. As objective as they believe they are, they will not cooperate with everyone in the same way. It makes a big difference who is asking them to change. If the manager is new or if the manager does not need the same strategies the team needs, it's imperative to prepare the manager to effectively communicate with doubtful analyst teams.

Authority and structure are very important to this team. Other than having a manager lead the process, it's also important to be very clear about the expectations, goals, and success criteria of the process with the doubtful analyst team.

When introducing a development process to any team or individual, it's always important to start by defining the goals correctly. While this is always important, it's specifically critical with the doubtful analyst team.

Doubtful analyst teams and individuals respond well to clarity as long as it's not in any way insinuating disappointment or criticism, so avoid debating what isn't working and focus on what you want them to achieve.

They respond well to a matter-of-fact outline of what is expected of them and they will make adjustments if they see consistency in the message and the way the message is communicated. Once needed strategies are acquired, this need for structure and the need to be right are minimized greatly. But at your starting point, it helps to start where the doubtful analyst is.

Finally, with doubtful analyst teams, it's important to start practicing the needed strategies almost immediately. Long preparation periods or explaining the need or value of a certain investment is not only futile, it's counterproductive. Get an agreement to start working with a certain solution in the absence of other solutions and stay focused on the desired outcomes. As long as doubtful analyst teams don't propose a different way to achieve desired outcomes, keep them accountable. If they do come up with a different way, allow them to test that new way, but create a clearly defined progress evaluation system that covers a long enough time frame to assure progress sticks.

Chase wanted to first reach an agreement with Stephan about the goals. Staying true to the process, forcing Stephan to jump into the solution until a better solution could be found, making it possible for both Stephan and Chase to move forward.

"I was initially concerned that Stephan would not want to cooperate with this solution. He wasn't excited about it initially or frankly at any stage, but the realistic approach to goals helped a great deal. I think the one thing that helped most was his sense that the process was managed with fairness...he knew we were trying to focus on his perspective too and that made a big difference. After five weeks, we started seeing great changes in how Stephan interacted with everyone around him. It took several more weeks to see the results applied to different tasks, but overall we could not be more pleased. The most wonderful thing is that being involved in guiding Stephan through the process meant I too benefited from the strategies. I now see these strategies everywhere in the organization." COO, biotech industry

It's important to understand that changing is always a choice. With people who don't want to change, there's always a chance that you won't be able to guide them through the resistance stage. Exiting resistance is a choice and no process can guarantee that people will always make a choice to change. We believe 90% is probably the best we'll ever be able to do.

The purpose of this process isn't to force people to change. As you'll see in Part Three, forcing change blocks people from accessing EBS, the system in the brain responsible for applying change in behaviors. Following the system, and engaging doubtful analysts in a way that takes into account how they operate, makes the teams who chose not to exit resistance the rare few rather than the more common response. The beautiful part is this response changes after the first strategy is acquired. With the new strategies in place, doubtful analyst teams no longer respond to the need to adjust or make changes in the same way they did in the past.

DO YOU KNOW A DOUBTFUL ANALYST TEAM, INDIVIDUAL OR ORGANIZATION?

Doubtful analyst teams:

★ Are reliable, respectful, extremely loyal, hard workers and typically ambitious, but not in a way that would contradict their values

★ Are charming, kind, very genuine and impressive with their sharp mind and level headedness, and if feeling appreciated will often present a balanced perspective

★ Can usually find excellent solutions to technical problems that others may have missed and are extremely innovative and methodical

★ Are generally brilliant and tolerant enough so they mostly adjust to external change relatively well, but are highly resistant when asked to change their behaviors

★ Have high standards and principles, strong personal convictions and intense sense of right and wrong that leads to many "shoulds" and "musts" which they expect others to follow as well

★ Will be quick to critique everyone and everything but don't appreciate being critiqued

★ Are rational and emotionally detached and often repress their own wants and needs through self-discipline

★ Often believe they know how to fix things, have very clear distinctions between right and wrong which creates rigidity and treating others with superiority

★ Will not be convinced by logical arguments if they disagree with your point of view, no matter how coherent you think your argument is

★ Are highly skeptical, generally dismissive and overall in disagreement, will stay away from generalizations and be very suspicious of the intentions of others

★ Will not apply changes without agreeing with the logic first and will not cooperate unless something makes sense to them

★ Often procrastinate and move slowly on projects, having a hard time starting new things because they feel everything must be done just right

★ Have a strong preference for using analysis and will only use synthesis for a limited number of tasks which makes them generally less flexible, open and inclusive

★ Appreciate authority, organization and structure

★ Often lack people management skills

GIVING DOUBTFUL ANALYST TEAMS ACCESS TO THEIR FULL POTENTIAL

Equip doubtful analyst teams with one to three of these strategies:

★ **STRATEGY #1: Synthesis Vs. Analysis**: giving doubtful analyst teams access to a more open, inclusive, intuitive, systemic view instead of thinking primarily in black and white, structured, methodical ways. This is important for effectively interacting with people, solving complex dynamic problems, moving from passive thinking to doing, removing procrastination, responding quickly to a changing environment, quickly making complex decisions, having more tolerance for ambiguity and more.

★ **STRATEGY #2: Multiple Truths**: an ability to allow contradicting truths to co-exist, openness to admit that people are not seeing the entire truth and that there can be different sides to the same situation or that people are seeing things incorrectly. This is important for effectively interacting with other people and specifically for team-work, agility, willingness to accept feedback, and for doubtful analyst teams to benefit from valid ideas by their quality regardless of the authority that can be assigned to the initiator of the idea.

★ **STRATEGY #3: Dynamic Hierarchy of Values**: an ability to flexibly evaluate, on an ongoing basis, the way our goals or values are defined in respect to needs in reality instead of rigidly following rules that may not apply in all situations. This is important in order for doubtful analyst teams to be more effective, efficient, notice more opportunities around them and further remove rigidity from interactions and decisions.

Additional highlights:

★ Avoid arguing with the doubtful analyst team, stay assertive, very clear about expectations and intentions and follow up on results.

★ Put the development of doubtful analyst teams in the hands of authority and preferably in the hands of another doubtful analyst that they respect and defer to, making sure this manager, facilitating their development, is in agreement with the steps that need to be taken.

★ Doubtful analyst teams respond well to clarity as long as it's not in any way insinuating disappointment or criticism. They respond well to matter of fact outline of what is expected of them and they will make adjustments if they see consistency in the message and the way the message is communicated.

★ Invest time in defining goals for the process with clear measurable criteria for success that take into account both your perspective and that of the team.

EMOTIONAL OSCILLATOR TEAMS

"WHAT DO I HAVE TO DO TO GET CONTROL?"

Succession planning is quickly becoming an important topic in organizations. According to an Oliver Wyman study, the National Association of Corporate Directors Public Company Governance Survey shows that board members rate CEO succession as one of their most crucial responsibilities. Perhaps a more telling fact is that they also rate this as one of the areas in which they are least effective. In the latest survey, only 11% said their companies were highly effective in this area, while 51% described their efforts as less than effective.

The same study indicates that some of the primary reasons for these results are selecting the best candidate for the job regardless of personal loyalties, coping with personal emotions, helping those not selected adjust and the ability of departing executives to move on.

It's often not a matter of knowing what the right steps are, or even which tools or models to use. It's most often a lack of execution of these models and tools as a result of mishandled emotions or misguided thinking.

Key Strategies are not the answer to all aspects of succession planning, of course. It's imperative to use the right models and structures. That said, a lack of certain Key Strategies plays a big role in the way succession planning, as well as other critical outcomes in the organization, are handled and executed. Teams with some clusters of strategies will deal with succession challenges better than others. The emotional oscillator cluster will probably have the most difficult time of all.

As you'll soon see, the main theme of emotional oscillator teams and organizations is control. Most changes carry a threat of change in control, which triggers extreme responses in emotional oscillator teams. Succession planning is one such change, other types of changes are included below.

Brian was managing a QA team for the third time, all in the medical technology industry. Before he had been a team leader and now he was the QA district manager. But in all his years, he had never ran into such a difficult team. He felt exhausted by the constant power games.

The QA department was made of five teams that worked in shifts to test the large machines. For some reason, the quality of the testing was below standard, and it was Brian's intention to make the necessary changes to establish excellent standards.

Initially it seemed like the QA teams had many genuine concerns. Brian tried making several changes to increase the department's productivity and satisfaction, including increasing the number of positions and changing the compensation structure. But it seemed like things only got worse.

"The team is made up of really difficult individuals. There

*are camps and sides and a lot of deceit going on. If you belong
to one camp you will do everything to sabotage the other camp.
I had many sleepless nights because of this department. At first
I thought it was because of the bonus structure. It was designed
in a way that made them compete against each other. But it's a
much deeper problem. Some people pretend to be working when
they are not, especially at night when there's no one watching.
All of this is hurting quality. Some of the team members act like
undeclared leaders. They have a lot of power and they know
it. As soon as a topic they are uncomfortable with comes up,
which is pretty much every other week these days, they start
overwhelming everyone else with exaggerations and outbursts.
They don't listen. Several meetings ended with someone being
literally aggressive, slamming a fist on the table or using other
threatening body language. In the meantime, quality scores
are plummeting, so this absolutely cannot go on...A couple of
months ago we had slight improvement when we let one of the
more dominant team members go. I'm not sure what to do at this
point."* QA District Manager, medical technology industry

Control in teams is often a complex thing. Many conflicts
in organization are fed by people's need for control and often
the formal definitions of who should be in control are not
aligned with who is actually in control.

The ineffective need to gain control in emotional
oscillator teams comes from the fact these teams lack very
specific strategies that prevent them from accessing their full
potential. The missing strategies make them lose control and
crave control in ways that don't benefit them and everyone
around them.

It's easy to identify the emotional oscillator team by
the emotional intensity of interactions and dynamics. The
team will go through a continuous cycle. As long as there's
no trigger for conflict or disagreement, the team will be
extremely productive, moving quickly to meet fast paced

goals. Typically things will be presented in the team with great excitement, even slightly exaggerated excitement. However, as soon as something triggers the team's resistance, it will go into a different mode. It will build up frustration and, at some point, experience an outburst of aggression that will be followed by withdrawal. The withdrawal will last until the team oscillates back to fast paced mode.

The expectations imposed on this team are for people to be doers with a lot of energy, inner drive and determination. The team will often jump to action very quickly. The moods in the team are often at extremes, as people are controlled by their emotions instead of the other way around.

They often don't effectively repress their aggressions and emotions, which often leads to big emotional arguments. Interacting with the formal or informal leaders of an emotional oscillator team often feels like watching a volcano about to erupt, at some point all hell breaks loose and then they seem exhausted, withdrawing into a shell of hurt or adopting other solitary responses.

Other people on the team will often feel uncomfortable about the way these behaviors are affecting others, including clients and colleagues or other people on the team. This can lead to gossip and lack of loyalty to leadership, especially in how the team is presented to others. It's common to talk to members on an emotional oscillator team and hear them say something like: "My boss will tell you we can do it in ten days, but you should really expect it in twenty days." The motivation of leaders in emotional oscillator teams is to gain control but ironically these teams are very much out of control. In fact, of the five clusters included in this book, fraud is probably most common in emotional oscillator teams.

In addition, as certain people on the team are looking to gain control over decisions in the team, other team members often respond by trying to avoid these outbursts, and this caution often costs the team in important areas like innovation. The team often avoids discussing disagreements, leading to faulty decisions and low engagement.

Emotional oscillator teams are curious, talkative, lively, and typically highly responsive teams. At least some of the people on the team are excellent presenters and sales people. They are excitable and can get very passionate about things they believe in or don't believe in. It's a team that focuses on doing, and leaders often feel as if things are not moving fast enough. It's not surprising that the biggest area of conflict in these teams is that leaders express a need for more control when the control they already have is overbearing and frustrating to others. Emotional oscillators will often define clear goals with great firmness but then neglect to follow up. They will often send mixed messages, treating incomplete tasks and insufficient progress as a disaster and a disappointment one day, and then behave as if all is well the next.

In their desire to move forward quickly, these teams often respond to new opportunities that take them off track. In this respect emotional oscillator teams are the opposite of doubtful analyst teams. The impatience of emotional oscillator teams will make them explore many things simultaneously, skip thinking and rush to action and implementation which often leads to redundancy and failing to successfully apply projects that require longer term investment and consistency.

A team is considered an emotional oscillator team not by the profiles of individuals on the team but by the dynamic in the team.

Sometimes some people on the team already have strategies that can complement the oscillator team by giving it the ability to move slower or more methodically, for example. However, the dynamic on the team prevents the team from accessing the abilities of these team members.

For Brian and his team, the need for control and difficulty controlling emotions led to unnecessary conflicts, resulting in low productivity, making discussions very difficult. Every topic seemed sensitive and it was nearly impossible to see a way to achieve desired outcomes without either giving in or starting a war that may result in losing key individuals. Unfortunately in such a knowledge intensive team, losing several key individuals can mean losing many months of critical production.

Emotional oscillator teams are often led by individuals who are uninhibited in their communication and actions, saying and doing whatever they think without any buffers. They tend to express things in extremes in order to convince and influence others, often using storytelling and presenting facts with an added layer of superlatives and drama. During conversations, they will often be overbearing, not knowing when to stop and listen. As a result, other people on the team will not share their opinions, ideas or concerns.

Emotional oscillator leaders can be highly demanding. In the extreme, they become offensive, manipulative, and insensitive when it comes to going after what they want. They will diminish and belittle others if it means getting others to understand their point of view and will often outburst in resentment if their point of view is not accepted. They typically tell themselves their resentfulness comes from not feeling valued and will just as easily turn from anger and belittling others to being deeply hurt.

The emotionality of this team is fed by what we can only describe as constant inner talk. Some of this talk builds up excitement and typically over confidence, but it also builds anger, driving the emotional oscillator team to faulty conclusions and decisions. This inner talk often builds emotional intensity that makes the emotional oscillator team blind to input about critical considerations they need to see.

Brian's team was informally led by team members who used extreme emotions to manipulate people around them and gain control. Expressing dramatic anger, hurt, and other negative emotions, several team members on Brian's team could become highly combative, confrontational, and intimidating.

When managers don't have access to effective tools for dealing with emotional oscillator teams, they frequently fall under the power spell of certain individuals on the team. This leads to lost control and an inability to guide the team to higher effectiveness.

To make things even more difficult, except for rare incidences, people who belong to this cluster will not admit their own weaknesses and will not negotiate in a reasonable way. Their cycle of outbursts and withdrawals make it impossible to engage emotional oscillator teams in a productive conversation about needed changes and adjustments they don't agree with. Logic and better explanations really don't do the trick here.

It's easy to see why managers tend to think of people who fit this cluster as difficult individuals, assigning their emotional intensity and responses to their personality, which managers believe cannot be changed.

Choosing a more moderate approach of calm conversation like Brian did, allows emotional oscillator leaders on the team to gain control. Choosing to fight fire with fire will make these individuals fight the manager to the bitter end. Successfully guiding emotional oscillator teams to exit resistance is an art form we have refined with great results. I'll go into what has consistently worked for us toward the end of the chapter.

In our experience, emotional oscillator teams can be changed with 90% success and in a lasting way if managers know how to address them correctly.

The personality people see is a representation of needed

Key Strategies. When the needed strategies are put in place, taking into account the deep resistance this cluster exhibits, people change, team dynamics change and desired outcomes are achieved. When the right Key Strategies are acquired, they replace a win-lose equation with a win-win equation.

It's very difficult to push people out of their comfort zone, but when you know how to transition people into a new comfort zone, they can see things like they have never seen them before.

For emotional oscillator teams, much like with other clusters, the key is to transition the team into a new comfort zone before asking to see a change in outcomes. As long as Brian tried working on quality issues and productivity issues without first establishing the new comfort zone and giving the team the Key Strategies it needed, the team resisted Brian and he couldn't get the team to make needed adjustments.

For Brian, low quality results meant multimillion dollar medical equipment went out to customers with unnoticed defects, exposing the company not only to future defect costs but also to risky lawsuits. *"This process allowed us to keep the same people but get them to have new personalities. Our QA department had some very strong personalities that took advantage of the new incentive program in a negative way. The assessment report identified the underlying conflict, but more impressively, the process got power struggles out of the picture, making the team work together to exceed standards. After 12 years in management I can say there's no other process out there, at least that I know of, that is quite like this process."* QA District Manager, medical technology industry

As I mentioned in earlier chapters, the strategies needed in order for teams to gain access to their full potential are exhibited in a variety of behaviors, and that of course includes how people resist. Once the right strategies are acquired, behaviors change. But even more importantly, for the lasting effect of the current change and future changes, the way people resist change is altered too.

THE STRATEGIES NEEDED TO SUPPORT THE EMOTIONAL OSCILLATOR TEAM

The Head of Cardiology in a children's hospital was pressured to accept our assistance in resolving the low satisfaction rates his department received consistently from customer satisfaction surveys. The hospital had no power to influence this senior doctor but hospital leadership made it clear they saw his management style as the primary factor contributing to poor results.

"...Doctor Baker is without a doubt one of the best doctors we have, but his teaching style and interpersonal skills are of great concern. The main issue nurses and interns bring up is his demeaning manor. Nurses feel many of their needs are unheard. They tell us Doctor Baker is dismissive, impatient, harsh and directive. He seems to yell at them and use derogatory terms. This is clearly not an environment that supports learning. When staff make mistakes, they often report feeling humiliated by the way solutions are presented, especially when it's done in front of patients. This of course affects patient satisfaction and level of care." President and COO, medical industry

When presented with requests to change in the past, Doctor Baker was disinterested in cooperating with any development efforts. His perspective was that the nurses and interns were not performing up to par and that they should not expect what he called "special treatment." He felt that some of the complaints interns and nurses brought up were ludicrous. He believed the overload staff experienced was due to their own performance quality. The assessment report showed that Doctor Baker felt underappreciated for his contribution and hard work, and the many hours he put in above and beyond to teach and guide interns and doctors in his department. In his own words, he was deeply hurt by the insistence to make him the bad guy. If it wasn't for his deep passion to give the best care possible to children, he would have given in his resignation a few years ago.

Unfortunately, because emotional oscillator leaders don't easily admit their own weaknesses or flaws, offering to coach Doctor Baker was met with a tall brick wall.

When pressed to the wall, emotional oscillator leaders are likely to accuse others, belittle others, get hurt, angry and defensive and threaten with extreme consequences. They will assert themselves powerfully to keep control or they will present a deeply hurt front and discontinue the conversation.

Though this wasn't the case with Doctor Baker, emotional oscillator leaders will sometimes pretend as if they are cooperating, but will sabotage making any progress in a variety of ways. The most common of which for emotional oscillators is to rush and apply things without thinking and without fully understanding what is required. This prevents them from having to stop and acknowledge their part which, like everything else with emotional oscillators, is all about control.

To bypass this initial resistance, it's important to be clear about the win-win solution, genuinely focusing equally on the emotional oscillator's perspective and needs and on the needs of the organization and the team as a whole.

The three strategies that allow emotional oscillator teams to optimize productivity, giving them access to their potential are:

→ Introspection and Emotional Articulation
→ Effective Control
→ Deliberate Proactive Choice

Key Strategies are hierarchical. Some strategies target a basic emotional response while others create effective thinking platforms. Introspection and Emotional Articulation is one of the strategies that are closest to the emotional core. Without introspection, people don't acknowledge they have any part in the problem and hence are impossible to change. Simply put, if people have no access to what they feel and how they process things, people will be blind to their contribution to the results they achieve. When that is the case, it's impossible to start any discussion about changing people. They will deny and reject any suggestion for needed change.

STRATEGY#1: INTROSPECTION AND EMOTIONAL ARTICULATION

This strategy reinforces pausing and evaluating if people are using Introspection and Emotional Articulation. It's important that strategies are not directive. Most strategies that direct people to do X or Y will fail and not be acquired in a lasting way by the brain.

This strategy does not direct people to express their emotions or to be introspective. It guides them to notice when they are and when they are not using Introspection and Emotional Articulation. This may seem like a minor detail, but as you'll see in Part Three, the way strategies are designed is of monumental importance.

Equipping people with the strategies they need in order to access their full potential is a true win-win. It's a gift of genuine empowerment for people on the team and it's an effectiveness building platform that leads to higher productivity and desired outcomes that benefit the team and the organization as a whole.

Once Introspection and Emotional Articulation is acquired, teams can understand how their emotions are affecting them and start developing a key to control their emotions.

STRATEGY #2: EFFECTIVE CONTROL

The main theme in emotional oscillator teams is control. Some people in the team get control while others relinquish control. This strategy gives people the ability to distinguish between Effective Control, the type of control that will make people cooperate to achieve desired results, forced control, and completely relinquishing control to other people. Again, the strategy isn't designed to push Effective Control over forced control. Work dynamics are complex, and no choice is always the right choice. As in all other strategies, both approaches are needed in different situations. Sometimes, forcing people to follow certain instructions is absolutely the right thing to do.

In Doctor Baker's case, one of the biggest challenges was overcoming the need to build trust. Doctor Baker didn't trust the hospital's leadership intentions, just as nurses and interns didn't trust Doctor Baker's intentions. Talking about trust with emotional oscillator teams is not the right way to go. Without the right strategies first in place, trust is just a hollow word and everyone in the organization knows it.

Emotional oscillator teams and leaders will initially not believe anything you say. They will not believe you genuinely want to help them. Teams will question the genuineness of the process and wonder if it's a disguised attempt to criticize or hurt them. This is one of the many places where the art of changing people who don't want to change comes into play, guiding managers and change agents, preparing them to overcome these and other predictable obstacles along the way.

Combining the right strategy with the right process, as well as guiding emotional oscillator teams through distrust and resistance, leads to the acquisition of this new strategy, transforming teams in a lasting way. Manipulation turns into a genuine give and take. Overbearing control turns into respect for other team members' needs. The team wins, the emotional oscillator leader wins, and the organization as a whole benefits greatly.

Effective Control further reinforces letting go of emotional outbursts because it removes one of the main reasons emotional oscillators lose control. Increasing people's ability to gain control through cooperation reduces frustration and obsession around gaining and keeping control.

This strategy is also linked to the rushed tendency emotional oscillator leaders and teams have. Because these teams are seeking control through doing, they are quick to jump to action, come up with new ideas or start many new initiatives to speed up achieving what they want. These reactions reduce the effectiveness of efforts that require consistency and make teams respond before they are ready, which results in losing opportunities that require more preparation.

It's rare, but in some cases, the first two Key Strategies are sufficient in order to create a deep transformation in emotional oscillator teams. For Doctor Baker, the two strategies made a huge difference. For the first time, he could see what he was contributing to the dynamic with interns and nurses. He could see a better way to achieve what he wanted, a win-win strategy he was comfortable using.

"The results were clear and unmistakable, achieved in a short time and we have every reason to believe the transformation will last. Seeing an executive change so quickly is a wonder…the most impressive thing is that the staff noticed the changes in big things but also in everyday things…we were not surprised to find that customer satisfaction surveys were showing great improvements as well." President and COO, medical industry

STRATEGY #3: DELIBERATE PROACTIVE CHOICE

Emotional oscillator teams, even when they can articulate

emotions and develop effective ways to gain control, are typically still unwilling to let go of blame and anger. They can be addicted to negativity and drama. The hidden reason for this anger comes from the fact that emotional oscillators feel they have given up control against their will. This third strategy breaks this tendency, allowing emotional oscillator teams to develop an internal center of control, let go of blame and negativity, and start building positive and proactive dynamics.

This third strategy adds to the first two and gives emotional oscillator teams the ability to look inwards, take responsibility for setting boundaries and stop the vicious passive aggressive cycle. With Deliberate Proactive Choice in place, emotional oscillator teams can be comfortable with vulnerabilities and open up to changing. Integrating these strategies makes it possible for emotional oscillator teams to create balanced and powerful forward movement. Being able to control their emotions instead of being controlled by them gives teams the ability to moderate their extreme responses.

While the cluster of emotional oscillator teams is relatively simple to identify by the intensity of the dynamics in the team, this profile can be deceptive.

To be confident a dynamic in a team fits the emotional oscillator cluster, it's important to look at behavioral patterns across a variety of situations and circumstances.

Emotional oscillator teams will move fast, get tasks completed quickly and will typically provide brilliant creative, practical solutions to even the most complex problems. When emotional oscillator teams are not under stress to change, they have tremendous energy, are engaging, extremely generous, and caring. When clients meet these teams in this zone, clients often receive a "wow" customer experience. Emotional oscillators will abandon their boundaries and give absolutely everything possible to clients, making them feel special and valued, providing services at a moment's notice. These teams are very focused on creating deep meaningful relationships with clients. They will be committed to the highest standards of professionalism, service, and execution.

Since emotional oscillator teams will react differently in different situations, it's important to see the complexity of the situation. Without fully exploring the patterns across different situations, emotional oscillator teams may at times be confused for the flamboyant or pleaser teams I'll discuss in later chapters. Flamboyant teams share the same intensity. Even pleaser teams can be similar due to their need to dismiss their own needs and focus on pleasing others.

Desired outcomes and Key Strategies have a lock and key relationship. The wrong cluster of strategies, even if acquired by teams in a lasting way, will not lead to desired outcomes.

Strategies that match specific behavioral patterns and dynamics are chosen because they have been shown to consistently allow teams to make needed adjustments and reach desired outcomes. The real criterion for the fit between a certain strategy and certain patterns in teams is consistent change in application. With the right Key Strategies, the transformation is successful, the change in emotional oscillator teams is identified by people on the team who needed to change, but more importantly, by the leaders who initiated the change and by other people independently interacting with that team.

THE EMOTIONAL OSCILLATOR TEAM BLOCKING DESIRED BUSINESS RESULTS

In recent years, CEOs repeatedly ranked innovation, self-renewal and reinvention among the top ten important areas to focus on year after year. A recent study by *Business Week Magazine* and the Center for Business Innovation and Creativity at Kennesaw State University shows that the main obstacles for innovation are mostly related to people. The highest contributing factor is perceived to be resistance to change. Additional obstacles are lack of time, fear of risk taking, and lack of creative skills.[8] A similar study presented in Europe this year highlighted skill constraints, lack of access to sufficient technological knowledge, and market knowledge as three of the top five innovation barriers across firm types and countries.

We have found that the best way to know if your team is equipped to innovate, among other desired outcomes, is to identify which Key Strategies are still needed for that particular team. For emotional oscillator teams, the control and emotional intensity of the team often block everyone but very few individuals in the team from being creative and innovative. Frequently, emotional oscillator leaders, formal or informal, will be very creative, but practice ineffective innovation since their ideas will lack the research and study provided by slower, more methodical progress. Other team members will not contribute ideas or help buffer the ideas of emotional oscillators, costing the business an additional important element of innovation. If you have ever tried to change a passive team that fears the responses of someone on the team, you know the full effect of the emotional oscillator cluster.

There are several excellent models and methodologies that define which type of skills and tools will lead to increased deliberate innovation. The ability to shift from focus to free flow thinking is one such skill, problem solving and looking

---

8   A Report Card on Innovation: *How companies and business schools are dealing with it*, Gary Selden and Harry Vardis, BusinessWeek Research Services and Center for Business Innovation and Creativity at the Coles College of Business, Kennesaw State University, 2010

for deep new insights is another. The problem is, without certain prerequisite strategies, teams can't start practicing new and needed skills. Other things in the team dynamics will block the team's access to practicing needed adjustments.

Innovation is of course one example. To get desired outcomes you need to start by getting people to acquire the needed Key Strategies, and you need to give people a system to acquire those strategies because most of the people on your team will resist creating the new needed synaptic pathways.

Alex spearheaded a cultural change in his industry. As a senior director of a large corporation in the manufacturing industry, he and his colleagues wanted to shift the organization from traditional top down culture to servant leadership culture.

"The new values we speak of will make a difference in people's lives. The departments and individual managers that have adopted the new values already see growth, higher productivity and less work-related accidents. It's very obvious that in teams that have developed new values, metrics are picking up. This transformation has put our corporation in the spotlight. Many leaders of other companies in our industry are eager to learn from our experience and success. The challenge we have is with several leading managers who find the new values foreign. Despite everything we tried, some people just don't want to jump on board. We'd like to see them join us." Senior executive, manufacturing industry

While other organizations wanted to learn all about Alex's progress, and although the results of the change spoke for themselves, certain senior executives and some managers were not willing to change their leadership style. Some of them have worked for the organization for over twenty years. Without a doubt, it's not an easy shift to make.

Initially, these executives and managers tried to conform to the new values, but soon more familiar behaviors returned.

One of the managers, Kevin, was a great example. Kevin was directive, highly task-driven, corrective, and controlling. He often lost his temper with his team during board meetings and with his colleagues.

Since the organization was measuring the results of the new culture in very tangible parameters, it was obvious that Kevin and other leaders in the organization were costing the corporation a lot of money in productivity and safety.

The issues Alex's corporation worked to solve are very commonly on the mind of CEOs and senior executives. Of these areas, CEOs rank as highest in importance, holding their business back from optimizing productivity and perhaps failing their organization in employee engagement, high executive burnout rate and high costs of CEO turnover rates. It seemed the organization defined a culture that worked beautifully for it in terms of reducing these prices, but despite the clear measurable results, certain people in the organization were not willing to cooperate.

There can be many other contributing factors for these results other than having emotional oscillator teams lack specific strategies. If teams fit this cluster, as they did in this case, there's a very high likelihood the organization will experience some of the above barriers to productivity and success.

Emotional oscillator teams often have to either allow controlling individuals to behave the way they behave, or they have to lose them. If it's just one individual that is using emotional oscillator patterns, it's sometimes better to replace that individual. When many people in the organization exhibit these patterns, it's often too difficult to do that.

However, there's a way to engage emotional oscillator teams and transform them, including their communication style, decision making processes, time management, project management, team dynamics, and other areas of concern.

It doesn't work by trying to break them. It doesn't work by trying to take control away from them. It works because it gives these teams prerequisite strategies that, when put in place, make it unnecessary for them to use the strategies they have been using in the past.

For Alex, the most important achievement was to create an effective channel for development and communication. Though it took a few months to complete the transformation, the impact of the new Key Strategies was noticeable and quantifiable.

"We are so impressed with this transformation, its wide impact and sustainability. This is particularly exciting because of the short time it took us to engage our people to use it. I have never understood what is at the heart of organizational change as I understand it now. This process not only allowed us to achieve the transformation we were looking to establish, it built our capacity to continually change and adapt throughout the organization." Senior executive, manufacturing industry

Of course, no solution is foolproof. People who are lacking certain strategies can always shut everyone else down and choose not to invest in achieving better results. The key isn't to prevent people from making a choice about changing. No process should force people to change. The key is a statistics game. The goal is to minimize the number of incidences in which initial lack of desire to cooperate prevents people from acquiring needed change and making needed adjustments.

To take 90% of people through this journey successfully requires familiarly with the specific strategies needed for each team. Leaders should understand the specific nuances required in order to guide that particular cluster through an acquisition process that takes into account the team's unique resistance and sensitivities.

GUIDING THE EMOTIONAL OSCILLATOR TEAM TO EXIT RESISTANCE

Todd was the coordinating director of a 12-man government research team. Each one of the researchers on the team had their own area of expertise. One of the researchers, Matthew, didn't agree with many of Todd's decisions and would occasionally walk out in disagreement or state he was not going to follow Todd's instructions.

"All I really want is an honest and open dialogue where new ideas can be explored and accepted. Researchers would understand the value and concept of mission assignment and leaders' intent. Matthew has related before that there was no reason for him to inform me of any activities. He will lose his temper and raise his voice at other team members and at me. Other times when I ask him to present something, he starts on an emotional rollercoaster, accusing me of not trusting him or limiting his independence." Director of Research, government industry

In many organizations, Matthew's behavior would have been sufficient justification for letting him go. That wasn't easy in this case. Todd was eager to find a way to resolve the situation. While Matthew was taking control, Todd was relinquishing control and the team as a whole suffered from this dynamic.

In order for emotional oscillator teams to change, people on the team must first change the way they resist. The controlling individuals need to develop more effective ways to achieve control, and other people on the team need to develop better ways to communicate with emotional oscillators.

The first step teams need to take is to gain a new, experience based definition of a new Key Strategy. Getting emotional oscillators to acquire the Effective Control Key Strategy for example, requires first getting the team to see

Effective Control, in the way we define it.

Building a new experience based definition requires overcoming the boundaries of words. When you describe to an emotional oscillator team what Effective Control means, the words you say and the way the team interprets those words will be different.

Defining the new strategies through experience will be difficult with emotional oscillators at first because they will take too much control, quick to think they know exactly what needs to be done before they truly listen to instructions. This means the response to a new definition will often be something like: "Yes, yes, I know exactly what you mean," when in fact the team or individual didn't grasp the new strategy. It's a lot like getting someone who sees green every time something is orange to see the difference between orange and green. Initially, they will be sure you are wrong and will say orange items are green, then gradually, by allowing their brain to be exposed to nuances they were not aware of before, they will develop enough distinguishing experiences to call green items green and orange items orange.

Creating a new experience based definition is difficult with any cluster anyway, but with emotional oscillators it's especially difficult because they don't take the time to see the differences between what they think you mean and what you actually mean.

Once a new experience definition is formed, it's an A-ha moment. For the emotional oscillator, this moment opens doors to an ocean of new possibilities, allowing individuals and teams to communicate without the emotional explosiveness, fast reactions and over decisive orientation for action that so often gets the team in trouble. As emotional oscillators start to develop the Key Strategies they need, they notice their emotions and can speak in subjective terms about their perspectives, making room for other perspectives and ideas, realizing they may be misinterpreting things and moving too fast to allow for resolutions. Their hurt response goes away, and they are then able to feel appreciated.

It's never enough to focus the change on one individual. The way people respond to that individual should also be addressed. As emotional oscillator patterns are replaced with more effective patterns, the team starts perceiving the change and, as the team interacts, other people start responding differently, allowing the team to build new lasting patterns.

Other than creating a new experience based definition, there are several other challenges for guiding emotional oscillators to exit resistance. As I mentioned earlier, trust becomes a huge issue, and it's particularly tricky because emotional oscillators will make it almost impossible for you to gain their trust.

The first thing to do is stop trying to get emotional oscillators to trust you before they acquire the strategies they need.

Working with emotional oscillator teams is a great example for the importance of not worrying about achieving commitment for change or building trust before jumping into practice. Emotional oscillator teams gain control by lingering in talking, asking questions and doing everything they can in order to retain control but at the same time they will not trust anything you say. The more talk there is, the less likely they will build trust. The only thing these teams trust is consistent actions. Don't be fooled by what they tell you or what they tell others about you. They may say you are the most amazing person, but they don't trust you.

At some point, relatively quickly actually, if you don't guide emotional oscillators to actions that will define the new Key Strategies correctly, emotional oscillators will start acting and making progress in the wrong direction.

To further support emotional oscillators overcome

resistance, find which benefits these individuals would have by changing, from their perspective. Emotional oscillators will often share those with you if you ask them. They very openly complain and talk about negative emotions. Focusing on their needs is an important first step. But be warned, once you hear their needs, you must leave their needs behind and get them to focus on desired results, both for them and for the organization.

For Matthew, the benefit was that Todd would listen to him more and integrate more of Matthew's needs into the way the office operated and tasks were handled. Also, if Todd would better understand Matthew, he would be able to give him more independence in running his projects. The condition and the desired outcomes Todd defined were that Matthew would be willing to work on the way he expressed himself with Todd and with the team.

Finally, another important challenge to overcome with emotional oscillator teams is preparing whoever is guiding the process to effectively handle the strong manipulative tactics of this specific cluster.

Typically, at some point during the definition of the new strategy, certain individuals on the team will resist in a most unpleasant way. It's important that managers are prepared for this and know how to respond.

How would you respond if someone attacked you or confronted you aggressively? Todd's mode was to try and find harmony. For Todd, conflict seemed unnecessary and when Matthew would launch at him, Todd seemed to accept it and try to bring Matthew back by asking for Matthew's cooperation. For Matthew, Todd's response triggered further distrust and disrespect. Other managers may have responded very differently when attacked. They may have responded with anger or frustration, making threats and focusing on trying to keep control.

When people deal with extremes, they tend to have extreme responses.

The most important thing about working with emotional oscillator teams is not to have any buttons. It's best to communicate with respect, with very clear explanations about what can and cannot be done, but without an emotional attachment. For many managers, this is easier said than done.

It was important to prepare Todd to lead the team as a whole, and Matthew in particular, through the natural resistance of changing, so that the change can be sustained.

"I'm now recognizing that I needed to change first. Clearly the strategies I used were not working with Matthew. He didn't trust me and despite my best efforts before, I could not reach him. Matthew recently expressed some concerns we were able to discuss and resolve and I made very clear terms for my expectations which he now respects. It no longer feels like there's a time bomb in our team. Disagreements are handled with respect." Director of Research, government industry

Understanding each cluster, its unique needs and nuances and its specific resistance responses, makes it possible to equip teams with new Key Strategies. It's then when new strategies are acquired in a lasting way, that teams can optimize productivity, and that organizations can access their full potential.

DO YOU KNOW AN EMOTIONAL OSCILLATOR TEAM, INDIVIDUAL OR ORGANIZATION?

Emotional oscillator teams:

★ Are curious, talkative, lively, and highly responsive teams

★ Take initiative, make things happen, have a lot of energy, inner drive and determination

★ Quickly become very close to other people, warm and affectionate but then can very easily get disappointed

★ Are excitable and can get very passionate about things they believe in or don't believe in

★ Will have emotional and intense interactions and dynamics, experience extreme emotions that often control them

★ Don't effectively repress their aggressions and emotions

★ Often withdraw into hurt after expressing anger

★ Avoid discussing disagreements until they can no longer hold back their emotions

★ Frequently change direction or try new solutions because they need to maintain a level of excitement and because they want things to move faster

★ Are excited about new opportunities, but don't follow through because of their impatience

★ Will often have to deal with control issues, as some individuals on the team will seek to achieve control in less than optimal ways and other team members relinquish control

★ Tend to jump to action before fully understanding or thinking things through

★ Often use storytelling and presenting facts with an added layer of superlatives

★ Can often be overbearing, not knowing when to stop and listen

★ Can be highly demanding and in the extreme become offensive, manipulative and insensitive when it comes to going after what they want.

★ Have a really hard time admitting their own weaknesses

★ Will tend to believe they are being wronged

★ Will prefer to avoid acquiring support or help from others

GIVING EMOTIONAL OSCILLATOR TEAMS ACCESS TO THEIR FULL POTENTIAL

Equip emotional oscillator teams with one to three of these strategies:

→ **STRATEGY #1**: Introspection and Emotional Articulation: giving emotional oscillator teams the ability to control their emotions instead of being controlled by them. This strategy makes it possible for these teams to break the passive aggressive, explosive-withdrawal cycle and communicate in a subjective way. They express their frustrations and needs in ways that others can understand and effectively respond to.

→ **STRATEGY #2**: Effective Control: allowing teams to develop a balanced interaction in which different needs are considered and thought through in order to achieve the goals of the team as a whole. The benefit of this strategy goes beyond communication. It gives teams access to better decisions, helping to buffer the need to move too fast, get more passive team members to contribute and use all the resources of the team.

→ **STRATEGY #3**: Deliberate Proactive Choice: facilitating teams to take responsibility, move away from anger, blame and fear into a cooperative< space. Among more obvious things, this strategy helps emotional oscillator teams with time management and project management.

Additional highlights:

★ Find which benefits they would have by changing, from their perspective and include those alongside very clear benefits from your point of view.

★ Pay close attention to the way emotional oscillators define the strategy in practice exactly as it's intended to be defined. Emotional oscillators tend to enjoy storytelling for the sake of storytelling and can lose the main point of the practice. They will often jump to action before they truly understand the main point.

★ Move to action as soon as possible and avoid lengthy explanations at first.

★ Make sure the system is set up not to allow certain individuals to take the stage only for themselves.

★ Get managers prepared for dealing with extreme resistance responses.

PLEASING TEAMS

"IF YOU ARE HAPPY, I'M HAPPY."

Ernst and Young's 2010 Business Risk report covering the top 10 business risks as perceived by senior executives, ranks talent management as the fourth most important risk to manage across 14 industry sectors. Acquiring talent and retaining top talent are becoming more important in many industries.

With top talent becoming such an important factor, there has been great focus on what employees want most. Studies highlight factors like autonomy, flexibility, innovation, collaboration, trust, and attention among other things. While clusters like doubtful analysts and emotional oscillators may lack in these areas, the pleasing team will be most successful at providing employees most of the desired factors. Where the pleasing cluster will run short is around other important factors such as building commitment to action, learning from mistakes and creating accountability.

The interesting part about pleasing teams and the number one reason I included this cluster in the book was because pleasing teams seem most cooperative, but struggle greatly with making needed adjustments. It's a fantastic example of people who say they want to change, who are open and cooperative, but who consistently don't apply needed changes in practice, certainly not in a consistent lasting way.

We tend to think of people who are eager to cooperate and please as people who are missing abilities like assertiveness or self-confidence but exhibit very low resistance. But when it comes to adopting more effective abilities, the pleasing orientation presents an important type of challenge. In fact, it can be one of the most frustrating clusters and it's the one most commonly treated incorrectly.

John walked into the team meeting wondering if today would be any different than any of the meetings in the last three years. His leadership team had agreed to make some changes and it would be wonderful if some of the guidelines they laid down last month were put to work.

He sometimes felt he was doing too much. Sure, he was the CEO, but the leadership team wasn't taking sufficient initiative. They were all very open and he believed they really cared about each other and the business, so he couldn't really understand their taking a backseat whenever he was in the room. Why was it that he constantly felt he needed to motivate them? Why didn't they make progress when it came to changes they agreed they would implement for the benefit of the team, but were so engaged when it came to client work? He truly believed the business would do much better if his leadership team was more proactive and assertive. As the CEO of a medium size company, John was eager to get his team of top performers to be more assertive and consistent, both with clients and internally.

"Everyone on the team is committed to our success, but for some reason we don't hold each other accountable for things we agreed on. When a deadline comes up, everyone will work

hard until the project is done, but in daily tasks, progress lingers. We have been fully aware of this issue and have tried to improve our interactions around follow up for a long time. Even though we are all committed to seeing the dynamics change, we are still seeing the same behaviors unchanged for years now."
CEO, IT industry

The telltale sign of the pleasing cluster is that it seems to welcome change but agreement is followed by non-action. Because of the nature of this cluster, the resistance often goes unnoticed, sometimes for years.

The predominant communication style of pleasing teams is relationship oriented, gentle, considerate, appreciative, caring, kind, thoughtful, encouraging, forgiving, and sincere. These teams tend to assign initiative to someone else, following gladly. However, despite their deep insights and understanding, and their ability to talk freely and with acceptance about how they need to change, they apply very little in terms of needed adjustments in a lasting way.

Pleasing clusters are very relationship-oriented, and it's very typical for leaders who belong to this cluster to include others, give credit and use words like "we" and "us." It's also common for this cluster to seek the answers outside of the team, as if there was a secret resource that they just need to access.

The relationship, care, and affection in John's organization were truly remarkable, but the leadership team was unable to execute on internal business and development plans that were agreed upon. Though the leadership team agreed on which changes would be applied in terms of interactions, procedures, structure, and otherwise, something was clearly holding the team back from implementing tasks.

Without anyone holding the sales team accountable, sales representatives, for example, didn't focus their time on sales exclusively. When someone on the leadership team didn't deliver on certain deadlines, no one followed up or held that individual accountable. The leadership team often over-promised, which periodically created tremendous pressure on the staff and often led to client dissatisfaction, despite the team's great efforts. The team didn't follow any clear structure, and with different team members coming and going at different hours of the day, the team was unable to coordinate and work to promote tasks together. However, the team has already identified all of these needed changes on its own. The real issue was they didn't follow up or follow through on making sure the needed changes were made.

When a pleasing cluster is the predominant culture in a team, people often respond inadequately to pressure, wanting to please everyone but at the same time forgiving everyone and accommodating others' needs, instead of holding people accountable.

The organizational price of pleasing teams is frequently translated into low sales and low overall productivity. As a byproduct, lack of progress often makes the leadership of pleasing teams push harder, talking about the need even more than before, creating more structures, more guidelines and getting more and more frustrated with each other. Some on John's leadership team started doubting if anything would ever change and if it didn't, they planned to move on, although they really liked the people on the team and considered them close friends.

Once the needed strategies were accurately identified along with the resistance types that make up the pleasing cluster, the leaders in the team learned how to quickly install the strategies and overcome the resistance. The team started implementing the tasks and results soon followed.

"This process seems to have worked with unexpected results and very suddenly. I came back from a business trip and found a

different organization. It's like something inside my team turned on and now it can never be turned off again." CEO, IT industry

Pleasing teams can be agreeable, accommodating, avoid conflict, unresponsive, and complaisant. They will prefer to sweep problems under the rug in order to avoid making other people uncomfortable, and will often say inconsistent things to different people in order to maintain the peace temporarily. As a result, they will have difficulty establishing priorities and making decisions. Pleasing teams will often not hold others accountable, will not complete things and will involve themselves with low priority tasks which will lead to insufficient planning and missed deadlines. They are this way not because they are lazy or incompetent. It's simply because they need certain strategies in order to access their potential.

The new strategies free team members from the uncontrolled need to make other people happy, giving the team the ability to balance boundaries, expectations and a drive for results with consideration and connection.

THE STRATEGIES NEEDED TO SUPPORT THE PLEASER TEAM

Pleasing teams are usually talented in many areas. They have great communication skills, an intuitive and perceptive understanding of people and complex situations, they are most innovative and creative, and they deeply care about each other. Organizations that fit this cluster often stay successful because of their high integrity and strong connections with clients, but their internal effectiveness and efficiency are typically lacking.

Pleasing teams are very different from both emotional oscillator teams and doubtful analyst teams in that their main focus is to be nice. They are highly attuned to non-verbal communication; they are optimistic, supportive, yet not overbearing in any way. They are excellent listeners, often to a flaw. People on these teams speak of each other with great appreciation even when criticism or improvements are needed. They let things that don't lead to desired outcomes linger, passively supporting a harmonious dynamic at the cost of needed adjustments. They try to reduce conflict and discomfort even at the cost of productivity and performances.

Julia was Michael's manager for more than two years and had great respect for his comprehensive thinking, especially when it came to solving complex issues. Michael was one of the team leaders Julia really wanted to see succeed. He was kind and considerate, and he was one of the only managers on her team she could strategize with, thanks to his deep understanding of systems and his strategic scope of thinking. However, other people didn't see him the same way.

"The team is frustrated with Michael's micromanaging during meetings. I was told more than once that the questions he asks and the things he tends to insist on are truly not relevant for the team at that moment. My experience with Michael is quite different. I often consult with him on complex problems and he asks excellent questions and can often come up with solutions no one else thought of...it would be wonderful to figure out where this discrepancy comes from and help Michael support his team in a way that will benefit everyone involved." Senior manager, insurance industry

To make the adjustments that would bridge the gap between Julia's perspective and the team's perspective, we first needed to identify which Key Strategies were needed for the team as a whole. The assessment identified that the best solution would be to give Michael access to three strategies, those that fit the pleasing cluster.

The three strategies that allow pleasing teams to optimize productivity, giving them access to their potential are:

→ Self Acceptance and Self Forgiveness

➜ KindExcellence™
➜ Synthesis vs. Analysis

STRATEGY #1: SELF ACCEPTANCE AND SELF FORGIVENESS

In essence, Self Acceptance and Self Forgiveness is the ability to treat oneself with respect and appreciation, moving quickly past any negative emotions that are associated to oneself. It will not lead people to arrogance; it's not a fake sense of confidence or self-glorification, quite the contrary. Nor will it make people avoid self-critiquing and learning; it merely takes away the emotional baggage that is associated with learning opportunities.

Pleasing teams come from a place of humility and are often self-diminishing. They define their emotions by how other people think or feel about them. Without Self Acceptance and Self Forgiveness as a foundation, it's impossible for them to change for a variety of reasons.

Firstly, as I will cover in more detail later in the chapter, this is because the need to please others postpones resistance, blocking change as a result. In addition, pleasing teams will want to focus on what they are doing wrong, dwelling in the past and in self-dismissal which makes it impossible for them to change. They come into the process with a high preference for being passive and following others, which further makes it difficult for them to acquire change.

STRATEGY #2: KINDEXCELLENCE™

This second strategy belongs to the same "family" of Key Strategies as Effective Control, one of the strategies needed for the emotional oscillator cluster. KindExcellence™ is the ability to balance the need for connection with the need to maintain boundaries, move toward goals and meet expectations.

Executives sometimes assume that managers should never be nice or build warmer relationships with their team if they care to get people to make needed adjustments. Pleasing leaders are a clear example that the other extreme is not the answer either. The right strategy is a balanced combination of both kindness and excellence, both caring about people and about business results and balancing the needs of others with clear boundaries that foster the success of the team.

Pleasing teams need to acquire KindExcellence™ so they can better set boundaries before they can benefit from applying other strategies.

STRATEGY #3: SYNTHESIS VS. ANALYSIS

When you met this strategy before, it served to equip doubtful analysts with the ability to effectively choose when to use synthesis or analysis based on the task rather than their natural tendency. While doubtful analysts prefer analysis, pleasing teams prefer synthesis and often confuse the two abilities, using synthesis when analysis is needed and vice versa.

Michael used both synthesis and analysis equally, but not in the right places.

Most people are more comfortable using either synthesis or analysis as their primary way of thinking. This Key Strategy creates a new way of looking at the world. Instead of letting what we are accustomed to using dictate our response, Synthesis vs. Analysis plants the ability to distinguish which situation requires analysis and which requires synthesis. The type of thinking is selected by the requirements of the task rather than by an autopilot response.

Michael micromanaged, using analysis instead of synthesis when he needed to allow free flow thinking and giving his team members the opportunity to deliver with independence and accountability. On the other hand, he used synthesis for tasks that required analysis. In certain instances, when the important thing was to stay focused and aligned, Michael would take the team off topic or distract the team into discussing non-critical aspects of the project.

It's possible for teams to gain greater mastery of synthesis or analysis before graduating to Synthesis vs. Analysis. It's then important to equip the team with other strategies such as Core Analysis or Systemic Thinking, but this wasn't the case with Michael's team. Michael already had a high mastery of both abilities, he simply didn't use them effectively.

Anecdotally, Synthesis vs. Analysis equally serves people who use mostly analysis as it serves people who use mostly synthesis. KindExcellence™, the previous strategy I discussed is another such example. It balances both people who focus mostly on kindness and pleasing as well as people who focus mainly on excellence and results.

This is important because oftentimes, two opposites will exist in the same team. When I discussed the emotional oscillator cluster, I pointed out that some people on the team needed more control while others relinquished control. Key Strategies are often designed in a way that supports the whole team in achieving balance. By getting a team to practice Effective Control, not only do people who need control start responding more effectively, those who have relinquished control start building a more effective relationship with control issues as well.

For Julia, Michael, and his team, the new strategies provided access to new dynamics and much greater productivity.

"The impressive thing about this solution is how fast it affected both Michael and his team. The team started noticing changes in Michael's performances in a matter of weeks and I can say without reservation that this is the single most impactful thing we could have done for Michael and the team." Senior manager, insurance industry

The pleasing cluster is not as common in organizations because frequently more dominant clusters, like emotional oscillators and doubtful analysts, take over. Generally speaking, the pleasing cluster is more common as an organizational culture in not for profit, government, services industry, research and small to medium organizations.

It would be wonderful to say that it's also common in highly effective and successful organizations in which the leadership depends on other talent in the organization for business progress. But, at least in our experience, this is not the case. Without KindExcellence™ and effective boundaries, leaders don't seem to be able to build a powerful business around them, even if they are joined by complimenting talent. When individuals that fit this cluster are in positions of influence, this cluster typically blocks the team in many undesired ways.

In leadership positions, people who need the strategies of the pleasing cluster will cost their team promotion opportunities, making decisions for the wrong reasons, increased overload as a result of taking on too much and an inability to solve conflicts. Trying to resolve conflicts when a team depends on a pleasing manager will feel a lot like swimming in place. The manager will listen, acknowledge the understanding of the situation, but then avoid dealing with it in any way possible.

Identifying the right cluster of needed strategies can be very deceiving. Pleasing teams are usually accepting, unpretentious, caring, imaginative, and creative, but under certain circumstances, especially if they are criticized by other colleagues in the organization, their passiveness will increase and they may become bitter or even outraged. They can turn petty, full of complaints and often childishly insistent when they feel disrespected and diminished.

THE PLEASING TEAM BLOCKING DESIRED BUSINESS RESULTS

Napoleon Bonaparte was quoted as saying that the secret to success lies in careful preparation followed by speedy and decisive execution. Speed is certainly one the important components when it comes to consistent execution. Reaching decisions effectively, getting quickly to the point, keeping short deadlines, and staying on the critical path are all important components of success.

While pleasing teams are highly attentive and quick to respond to specific requests, they typically lack the above behaviors. It's harder for pleasing teams to stay on track with their priorities and tasks. They are likely to spend valuable time in meetings, talking to people at length; they will often not delegate enough and take too much on themselves to begin with.

Nina was responsible for one of the seven Philippines regional teams Wayne was in charge of. Nina was very eager to be promoted, but Wayne didn't feel Nina was proactive enough. He didn't feel she took initiative where needed and he didn't feel she sufficiently understood how to lead a team to business results.

"Nina needs to drive her own growth and development. She needs to stop expecting others to spoon-feed her. If she wants to be promoted she needs to recognize it's not about others liking her or saying all the right things. It's about results. She misses the fact that if she gets the business results, she will get the accolades she deserves." Senior executive, telecommunications industry

When asked about her decisions or about things she presented, Nina often responded with a certain degree of insecurity and defensiveness, either going into long explanations and trying to show she didn't make a mistake, or quickly stating that she understood the need, trying to stop the conversation.

Managing virtual teams in different geographical locations is very common in today's global business environment. The clients we work with are frequently presented with interesting challenges due to the important role of management and the difficulty of supervision in such work environments. Dealing with change, distance and multi-cultural teams present unique technical concerns as well as other challenges.

When managers are not in the same physical location with teams, defining goals and following up on progress requires attention to new dimensions of distance and time. In global teams, results must be noticed by other people and change processes must always be supplemented with well-defined success criteria and evaluation.

It's even more important to get this type of feedback from people that interact with an individual or a team that needs to change if there are multiple cultures involved, especially with a pleasing cluster. People that need the strategies of the pleasing cluster will try to present things exactly as they believe their manager wants to hear them. They will do everything to put their manager's mind at ease, including presenting things in ways that are not fully aligned with reality. These responses don't come from a desire to sabotage the results; they come from a genuine need to maintain harmony and peace.

Pleasing teams often try to ignore or avoid anything that can cause a discomfort for others which frequently results is poor decisions. These teams are usually overloaded and under productive. They over-promise and under deliver, ironically, almost guaranteeing that someone will be disappointed with them. Wanting to make sure others are happy and not making decisions often slows these teams to a halt because systems usually have conflicting interests which pleasing teams don't try to resolve.

Interestingly, pleasing teams can potentially rank high

on many success criteria. They can be highly focused on customer satisfaction and loyalty, they are most flexible and adaptable when it comes to short-term requests, they are highly innovative and creative and they will follow regulations or other technical requirements with dedication. The part that is missing however is critical. Pleasing teams typically don't achieve excellence in execution because their priorities are often not aligned with the goals of the organization.

The process of acquiring needed strategies, as I will discuss in great detail in later chapters, has no limits of culture or distance. Under the right conditions and with the right structure in place, it can be as effectively managed overseas as it is when people are working in the same office. Managers have to stay connected to their teams regardless of this process in order for teams to be effective. If that communication channel is not yet established, working through this process will establish it, which in our mind is an added bonus.

Once Nina acquired the Key Strategies, she could truly understand the transformation she was required to make.

"Working with Nina through case studies that were a good fit for where she is coming from but also clearly exposing her basic assumptions, made it seem like we are looking into Nina's mind. It was as if we had the ability to see how her brain was wired and then, together we could rearrange things to build new meaning and new definitions. I have never seen a program so transformational work as deep as this program and with such a quick turnaround. Using the examples and stories is not intrusive, that would be a problem with some cultures." Senior executive, telecommunications industry

Without certain strategies, people are not aware of what's blocking them and cannot get out of their own way.

GUIDING THE PLEASING TEAM TO EXIT RESISTANCE

The resistance of the pleasing cluster is the most positive and elusive of all resistance types. Pleasing teams will seem most cooperative and motivated, and yet they will not apply needed adjustments in a lasting way.

With the pleasing cluster, it's important to be cautious and realize that the initial excitement may be a result of wanting to please the boss or even please an outside expert. The risk there is that the change will quickly fade away after a short time.

For this reason, introducing needed strategies without overcoming the resistance of the pleasing cluster doesn't promote success. The fact the resistance of pleasing teams seems so positive, yet doesn't lead to change, frustrates everyone involved, often including the people who are trying to change themselves. They believe they want to improve but for a reason that escapes them, they cannot.

Leaders in this culture are typically highly effective in identifying the processes, procedures, structures, or systems that would lead to desired results, but are often incapable of breaking away from awareness and moving into action. In fact, pleasing teams will dig deeper and deeper trying to understand what's wrong with them, which only reinforces old strategies further, making it even more difficult for these teams to acquire new strategies.

Trying to support pleasing teams to adopt new strategies is often the equivalent of you shouting out to someone "you can do it..." as they constantly tell themselves "I can't do this." Encouragement doesn't work when people believe they can't. Pleasing teams focusing on old strategies, further reinforcing what they have been practicing in the past, blocks the acquisition of new strategies.

On top of that, pleasing teams often don't perceive

themselves as resistant and they believe that if they want harder, they will move into implementation. This forced version of change makes it difficult to engage EBS and further keeps pleasing teams in awareness rather than in practice. Because the attempt to change is done through awareness, pleasing teams keep trying again and again but the implementation is sporadic, maintained only temporarily at best, until the strength of awareness fades.

When the strategies needed for the pleasing cluster to be effective are combined with treating the resistance of the pleasing cluster correctly, goals are quickly achieved. When resistance is treated correctly, acquiring new abilities around holding other people accountable and feeling comfortable with sustaining other people's discomfort becomes much easier.

Michelle was new to the business. As an HR Director, she felt truly fortunate because the owners of the organization appreciated her opinion and were willing to let her focus on developing the organization strategically in a way tied to the business goals, not just to typical human resources items like recruiting and compensation.

For the last four months, Michelle invested her time developing guidelines and improvement items for each of the business departments. She was thrilled by everyone's cooperation and openness. It wasn't anything like her previous job where people tried to present a front. Everyone in production, management, administration, and sales were completely transparent about their areas of strength and were very open about their improvement needs.

Michelle's organization, a medium size manufacturing company, wanted to make a decision about a new way to increase sales and customer satisfaction. They were exploring everything from developing a new product to developing a new market but their production line had not executed recommendations and decisions made in the past. Michelle felt that while the leadership team was excited about creating new opportunities, the production floor wasn't ready to take on such an initiative.

"Our organization is all about a familial culture. The leadership team is very close to everyone in the plant. They know each and every employee by name and they really care about people. The team is highly motivated, highly invested in improving things around here....The problem we see is that work procedures and processes are insufficiently clear to everyone, so the guys on the floor make many mistakes and waste resources. We have interviewed staff and presented them with very clear procedure and process changes but our measurements still indicate lower standards than we aim to achieve." HR Director, manufacturing industry

Organizations often see very clearly what the end result needs to look like in order for the organization to achieve its goals. What they are often blind to is how to get people to make the adjustments that are needed in order to get there.

That's not always the case. Sometimes certain team members see the answer while others don't. Other times, the answer requires everyone's input and a new way to look at the challenges. In this case, the needed changes were defined meticulously but people didn't align themselves with the solution, and the leadership team didn't know how to get people on board.

The assessment report, looking both at the solution as defined by the organization's leadership and at the needed strategies, pointed to clear characteristics of the pleasing cluster. The teams in this organization were lacking certain strategies, those of the pleasing cluster and that led to the passive response and to the inability to apply change.

Getting teams to apply needed adjustments wasn't achieved by convincing teams that procedures and regulations were important. Increasing importance or providing logic does not increase execution with this cluster. It wasn't done by focusing on motivating people or offering rewards. This organization tried several of these approaches before without consistent progress. It was achieved by overcoming the resistance of the pleasing team that prevents access to movement toward action and improvement.

It's often hard to overcome the resistance of pleasing teams because this type of resistance does not push back in the same way other clusters do. These teams resist by agreeing without making any decisions or choices. They simply agree in order to avoid rocking the boat. Because of the way the brain works, resistance is required in order to acquire a new strategy. Resistance elicits choice and since the pleasing cluster avoids typical resistant behaviors, it avoids choices and action.

The best way we found to overcome the resistance of the pleasing cluster is to allow non-action to come to the surface as soon as possible and then treat it as resistance, forcing pleasing teams to make a series of action-based choices.

With pleasing teams, it's important to avoid educating, motivating, or creating urgency around the need for deliverables. That will only increase the dependency on authority and guidance instead of getting pleasing teams to take ownership and initiative. Disappointment with their non-action response is equally ineffective for the same reason. These common approaches to dealing with pleasing teams are actually counterproductive when it comes to giving them access to their full potential.

To acquire the new strategies, pleasing teams need to take responsibility and take initiative themselves. All of the above responses take the responsibility away from them, making them follow again instead of building a new ability.

Michelle experienced the cooperative resistance of the

pleasing cluster. Cooperation without execution lasted for a while before Michelle encouraged resistance to surface. It was only once the right strategies were acquired in combination with eliciting resistance that change was noticeable.

"We finally see people getting the importance of procedures and regulations. It seems like until now everyone had their own idea of how things should be done and now we are all working in the same direction completely aligned. Now that we have our quality under control we look forward to creating new opportunities." HR Director, manufacturing industry

The way the brain works and, in particular, the way the EBS works, dictates that in order for change to be acquired into practice, experience must be initiated by the people who need to change. This is always true, but particularly important for pleasing teams. The passivity of the pleasing team and the fact that they avoid initiating is one of the trickiest resistances to understand and overcome. Being equipped with this understanding from the onset of a change process allows managers to facilitate their team to desired results easily and seamlessly, where before change was a long frustrating journey.

DO YOU KNOW A PLEASING TEAM, INDIVIDUAL OR ORGANIZATION?

Pleasing teams:

★ Have great communication skills, they are highly attuned to non-verbal communication, have an intuitive perceptive understanding of people and complex situations

★ Are relationship-oriented, gentle, considerate, appreciative, caring, kind, thoughtful, encouraging, forgiving, and sincere

★ Are most innovative and creative

★ Are optimistic, supportive, yet not overbearing in any way and are excellent listeners, often to a flaw

★ Seem to welcome change but agreement is followed by non-action

★ Can be accommodating, conflict avoidant, unresponsive and complaisant, sweeping problems under the rug in order to avoid making other people uncomfortable

★ Tend to assign initiative to someone else and have a high preference for being passive

★ Will typically want to focus on what they are doing wrong, dwelling in the past

★ Often respond inadequately to pressure

★ Will have difficulty establishing priorities and making decisions

★ Will involve themselves in low priority tasks which will lead to insufficient planning and missed deadlines

GIVING PLEASING TEAMS ACCESS TO THEIR FULL POTENTIAL

Equip pleasing teams with one to three of these strategies:

★ **STRATEGY #1**: Self Acceptance and Self Forgiveness: giving pleasing teams the ability to move quickly past any negative emotions they associate with themselves. This strategy makes it possible for pleasing teams to develop the confidence required for them to trust their own decisions, make mistakes and initiate action.

★ **STRATEGY #2**: KindExcellence™: equipping pleasing teams with the ability to balance the need for connection with the need to maintain boundaries, move toward goals and meet expectations. For pleasing teams, this strategy is the foundation for assertiveness and high productivity.

★ **STRATEGY #3**: Synthesis Vs. Analysis: this strategy gives pleasing teams the ability to distinguish which situation requires analysis and which requires synthesis. Pleasing teams tend to be in synthesis, being inclusive and open to a variety of different alternatives which at times blocks them from making choices and moving forward efficiently and effectively.

Additional highlights:

★ Avoid educating, motivating, or creating urgency around the need for deliverables. That will only increase the dependency on authority and guidance instead of build pleasing teams to take ownership and initiative. Disappointment with their non-action response is equally ineffective for the same reason.

★ Realize that the initial excitement of pleasing teams may be a result of wanting to please you or even please an outside expert. The risk there is that the change will quickly fade away after a short time.

★ The best way we found to overcome the resistance of the pleasing team is to allow non-action to come to the surface as soon as possible and then treat it as resistance, forcing pleasing teams to make a series of action-based choices.

FLAMBOYANT TEAMS

"NEW AND EXCITING THINGS ARE BETTER"

In a survey by the American College of Healthcare Executives (ACHE) three of the top concerns CEOs shared for 2010 were healthcare reform implementation, patient safety and quality of care and patient satisfaction.

Key Strategies are a hidden layer of factors that influence the above results. In every case it's people who design solutions, plan how to execute them and it's people who at the end of the day deliver or not.

You can look at strategic needs like patient safety and quality of care and break it down to systems such as: the use of safety practices and protocol, or the practice of procedures that increase effective, patient centered, timely, efficient, and equitable care.

There's ample knowledge and tools that outline exactly which procedures need to be followed and yet safety and quality of care are perceived by CEOs among the highest obstacles that need attention. These highlight the important gap between knowing which practices need to be adopted and the practices that are applied in actuality. At an extreme, it's the difference between having a plaque of organizational values on the wall and having people practice those values every day.

Flamboyant teams are wonderfully warm, socially skilled and fun to be around. Healthcare teams that fit this cluster bring life and energy to interaction with patients. They are highly focused on patient care and typically get raving reviews for the genuine support they provide.

When it comes to reform implementation on the other hand, flamboyant teams will lack in attention to detail and consistency. They will focus on people and relationships and will maintain a great environment, but they will fail to follow through or take care of the "little" things.

Flamboyant teams are stimulating and constantly focused on having a good time and enjoying life. In contrary to the doubtful analyst team, the flamboyant team will enjoy exploring things widely but not deeply. This tendency to know a little about a lot sometimes leads to making preventable mistakes. They enjoy living in a space of options. They don't like to be directed. They are drawn to new experiences so much that they will sometimes have faulty decision making processes that stem from the need to make changes for the sake of change alone. Their communication style is uninhibited, as team members say and do whatever comes to mind. These teams solve problems with great haste from a place of being unable to postpone gratification or withhold satisfaction. If there are problems or conflicts, they will direct all their attention to the problem, dwelling in it childishly to rid themselves of unpleasant feelings or they will ignore the problem completely and go on with their "everything is great" attitude.

The positive environment around flamboyant teams is often put to the test when the tension around the need for results and accountability increases.

They are typically brilliant teams that invest discussion time on the big picture. They are highly professional, articulate and efficient, but they don't attend to the details of application because they dismiss monotony and minutia. However, they can be detail-oriented if they must and even be excellent at it for short periods of time. They are highly practical, but only focus temporarily until they get excited about the next thing. Flamboyant teams love to learn and experience new things.

Much like the pleasing team's attitude is misleading, it may seem like the attitude of flamboyant teams toward change would make it easy for them to make needed adjustments. Surprisingly, most flamboyant teams are actually very difficult to change.

Susan was the VP of HR at a large IT corporation. Nine months earlier the organization decided to bring all of its independent sub-units under one roof and under one brand. From an HR perspective, this was an exciting challenge. The company hired marketing experts to communicate the change both to clients and to employees, and Susan was responsible for creating a comprehensive culture and support the smaller units in developing a sense of belonging to a bigger company.

"I guess you could call this a merger... Our goals for the transition are to increase customer loyalty and sales, and we understand that to do that the new units need to adopt our culture. We are also hoping to retain top talent by increasing the number of offerings we have as a bigger operation... There are many more career development opportunities now and we have in place systems to serve this purpose. We also want to increase inter-organizational referrals so that clients who get one service from us will have access to additional services internally." VP of HR, IT industry

The many goals Susan outlined are very typical for the flamboyant team. It's very common for flamboyant teams and organizations to have multiple goals and areas of focus. People in this cluster are often multi-tasking, going back and forth between many different areas of focus because they enjoy the synergy of working on multiple things simultaneously. They get bored focusing on one thing at a time.

The culture of Susan's corporation was very different than the culture of some of the sub units. While the CEO and leadership team were constantly creating new opportunities, changing and growing, some of the sub units were more methodical and slow moving. In fact, part of the reason the organization had so many sub units to begin with was because they began so many initiatives over the years.

The original autonomy of the sub units created a successful relationship between the flamboyant corporation and the more structured sub units. Now, however, the benefit of uniting them brought about a need to solve some new issues.

Managers in the business units had access to the organizational values and the new systems that were designed to increase internal referral and career development, but this new culture wasn't adopted by some of the sub units and the systems were not used. Too many cross sales opportunities were missed and too many top talent employees left despite the fact there were good opportunities in other parts of the merged organization.

The assessment report highlighted that in this particular case, lack of execution didn't stem from resenting the merger, from lack of attention to detail, or from politics and contrasting interests. The core reason managers and teams didn't use systems and procedures in a way that led to achieving goals was because they were missing very specific Key Strategies that fit the flamboyant cluster.

The needed strategies are often not descriptive of the entire organization. In fact, they are not descriptive at all.

A descriptive assessment would have highlighted the clear differences between the culture of "headquarters" and the culture of the indigent sub units or perhaps even the specific strategies each individual team was lacking. The assessment we use doesn't aim to describe, it aims to solve an existing gap. Instead of asking how the teams are different, the assessment we use focuses on which Key Strategies, if practiced by the right people in the organization, would allow the organization to achieve desired outcomes on its own.

The core solution needed in Susan's organization was for both the integrated units and leadership to see the whole picture, with the different details that went into the new entity. The leadership seemed to skip noticing the impact the transformation had on the previously independent units. The managers of the independent units failed to focus on how their units fit the bigger scope of the business. It's of course not obvious that teams would adopt new ways of reacting even if assessments identify the right strategies. Assessment tools must be combined with the right acquisition system. I will elaborate on the system we use in Part Three. Once the needed strategies, addressing the core solution the organization needed in order to achieve desired outcomes, were acquired by every last employee, they led quickly to a transformation and desired results.

"It really was the job of our managers to get teams on board but they didn't have the tools to get people where they needed to be. Getting access to this important new knowledge made the transition seamless. With the new abilities distributed to all, on a cellular level, we started seeing a clear shift. In four months client loyalty and referrals were increased significantly and our retention program is very successful. It's a highly recommended eye opening solution." VP of HR, IT industry

Organizations don't have control over many things that affect their success. The one thing they can and should impact is people.

THE STRATEGIES NEEDED TO SUPPORT THE FLAMBOYANT TEAM

Flamboyant teams often start with a big burst of energy but then fade away without any results. Some startups fail because they're based on the leadership of very charismatic individuals who belong to this cluster. These teams would have benefited greatly if they had more methodical or analytical members on their teams, and if they allowed for a balance between their swooping energy and new initiatives and the slower thinking, careful progress of others.

Without those boundaries, flamboyant teams typically create great flames that burn fast.

Catherine managed a database team and was asked to design a system and train hospital personnel to use the new data management system. She spent many hours meeting with senior and junior staff to design a solution that would best serve them. Unfortunately, the system wasn't used, so it couldn't prevent human errors as planned. *"The most frustrating thing is constant changes to original requests. It seems every time I come in to present the senior staff with the system, new needs come up."* Head of Systems Development, medical industry

Initially, Catherine thought the changes were minor, but gradually she came to expect new needs and delays in application, until the system was completely abandoned.

Getting teams to adopt new technologies is typically not an easy thing. There are objective challenges involved such as switching from an existing system to a different system, or devoting time to getting used to the new system when it's logistically difficult. With the flamboyant team the difficulty level increases because of this cluster's lack of desire to settle on anything permanent.

In addition, because flamboyant teams don't pay sufficient attention to detail, they often discover needs for changes as they go. This impacts other departments or people who need to work in alignment with flamboyant teams. What may seem to flamboyant teams as minor adjustments, or exciting new discoveries, often translates into many hours of work for people around them.

The three strategies that allow flamboyant teams to optimize productivity, giving them access to their potential are:

→ Postponing Judgment
→ Global Optimization Vs. Local Optimization
→ Systemic Thinking

STRATEGY #1: POSTPONING JUDGMENT

This Key Strategy slows down the decision making process, forcing people to evaluate their reasoning and assumptions before jumping to action.

In Catherine's case, working with a flamboyant team was like working with a moving target. The team responded to any new idea, wanting Catherine to implement it to improve the system. The constant need to improve made it impossible to start implementing anything, and more importantly, this prevented the team from reducing the errors the system was designed to prevent.

STRATEGY #2: GLOBAL OPTIMIZATION VS. LOCAL OPTIMIZATION

Some people prefer to optimize locally, looking to establish solutions for immediate needs while other people prefer to look at the big picture and pay prices in the present as an investment for better results in the future.

An effective use of this strategy is deciding which of the two optimizations to choose based on the task at hand instead of by cultural or individual preference.

This strategy will help in a variety of situations, including flamboyant teams. Flamboyant teams typically create big plans that lack in detail and then they have a clear preference for local optimization. They will want to solve problems that are discomforting them in the here and now instead of building a detailed, long-term plan to solve the problem from its root. They will tend to prefer the urgent to the important, leaving very little time for long term solutions.

In Catherine's case, the teams she worked with didn't want to make the time to train and use a new system. Making those changes increased their short-term load and they preferred to avoid the short term work, despite the fact that it prevented them from overcoming an important long term price.

STRATEGY #3: SYSTEMIC THINKING

Flamboyant teams are focused on their own needs and wants. They often don't take into account the consequences and implications their actions and decisions have on other teams or on other parts of the system.

Sometimes, this tendency is moderated once the first Key Strategy, Postponing Judgment, is acquired. Other times, all three strategies are needed.

The goal of reducing human error by using a new system requires teams to make certain adjustments. It requires that people stop coming up with new needs and ideas, and, instead, understand and respond to the implications their actions, or lack thereof, have on the system.

Once senior staff members guided junior staff members in acquiring the above three strategies, the interaction of teams in Catherine's organization with the new system changed. *"The great value we gained from this process was people understood the importance of following the training. There was nothing wrong with the system itself but there was something stopping teams from using it correctly. It was a relief everyone finally cooperated. We have been struggling with it for a while. Now there are minor modifications needed like with any new system but it no longer feels like an uphill battle."* Head of Systems Development, medical industry

The specific strategies needed for teams, and the order they need to be acquired, are identified not only by the patterns in the team but also in respect to the specific goals the team needs to achieve. A team that needs to focus on adopting a new technology may need a slightly different emphasis than a team that has an urgent conflict to resolve.

There are many factors about change that organizations have relatively little influence on. Changes in the market and the need for new technology are two such examples. While it's difficult to influence external factors, influencing the way people respond to those changes can and should be made much easier.

THE FLAMBOYANT TEAM BLOCKING DESIRED BUSINESS RESULTS

Flamboyant people promoted to senior executive positions who have created a balanced environment around them, will very likely be extremely successful. Flamboyant organizations, because of their great flexibility, typically have the capacity to deal with increasing uncertainty, globalization and innovation. They are usually familiar with the most recent technologies. When they depend on solid decision-making processes, with the aid of effective analysis, they will make excellent decisions. The problem is, most flamboyant teams don't value analysis and structured systems sufficiently to accept support in those areas. With flamboyant leaders at the top and the lack of sufficient follow through, organizations will often deal with challenges like implementing new regulations with very little success.

The over flexibility and the frequency of change in

flamboyant teams often make it difficult for these teams to optimize productivity and access their full potential.

As the owner of a small recruiting company, Arnold was extremely passionate about running a tight team that performed at top quality at all times. Arnold's company provided services to government offices as well as to a variety of small to medium size companies in high-tech and finance industries. Though the success of the company was consistent, Arnold felt company growth was too slow, especially in comparison to the growth of direct competitors. *"Developing our business to meet market standards requires much greater flexibility. Most of the time we are moving at 50 mph when we should move at 80 mph. The most important goal right now is to dream bigger and quickly implement the needed changes so we can meet those bigger goals."* Owner, services industry

The assessment report identified that Arnold's team was missing the three strategies of the flamboyant cluster and that it was actually too many changes that were blocking the organization's growth, not insufficient changes.

The team operated on coming up with new ideas, implementing them, then evaluating them and making adjustments. With a methodical doubtful analyst team, this process, though slow, would have created focus and refinement. In a flamboyant team, like Arnold's, evaluation led to new ideas, not to refinement.

Needed strategies are often not the direct answer to the team's questions. They are the foundation for the team to identify the right answers and make needed changes on its own. In this team's case, the solution wasn't to tell Arnold's team which initiatives to choose; it was to help the team acquire the strategies that would get them to think more methodically and effectively about opportunities and new initiatives. This is important because without certain strategies, flamboyant teams will not follow the best advice. Even if they agree, it will only take a few months before they become enamored with a new, exciting idea without sufficiently assessing its applicability. They will often interrupt the consistency of other efforts that need more time to mature.

Due to the low follow through, team members developed a passive response to Arnold's expression of urgency. When a team notices that many plans are made but most are not followed through, people tend to disengage. They stop investing in the new thing because they have come to expect that effort will be interrupted soon by another effort. When this happens, flamboyant teams become extremely dysfunctional.

This in itself may increase turnover, another common side effect of flamboyant teams. In small organizations like Arnold's, when the culture is dictated directly by the owner, and as people become more passive around the flamboyant leadership, low productivity often leads to terminations.

Imagine the Queen of Hearts, impatient and dissatisfied with the lack of energy, accuracy, or otherwise deliverables of her team walking around and shouting "off with their heads." Flamboyant people in leadership positions will try to bring up the need for change a few times before losing their patience. They will not provide clear improvement notes and will kill motivation and engagement by not being consistent enough, but since they are blind to all of that, they will constantly express their frustration with the team's involvement. At some point leaders who lack the strategies of the flamboyant cluster will be very frustrated with people not "getting it" and will reach a boiling point very similar to the Queen of Hearts.

Without the needed strategies, Arnold's organization didn't have access to the team's potential. Without first developing strategies to respond more effectively, the team didn't want to change because it couldn't change. *"The process was truly transformational. I feel the team understands me now better than they ever have and I have a much better understanding of what they need from me in order for us to grow to new heights. Not only did the process open our eyes to the changes we needed to make, it made it possible for us to achieve our goals as a team."* Owner, services industry

Though this wasn't the case in Arnold's team, flamboyant teams are often distracted and though they can be inspiring and excellent promoters, they often don't deliver with equal quality. When entire organizations share this type of culture, the organization will often be very successful in terms of sales and marketing. However, sales teams in such organizations will often promise more than the organization can deliver, leading to conflicts with R&D and production.

You would think that because flamboyant teams are so fond of new things they would be excellent at making needed adjustments, but nothing could be further than the truth. Flamboyant teams are impatient and deeply dislike being directed or instructed. They love changing when it's their idea or their initiative, not when it comes from others.

GUIDING THE FLAMBOYANT TEAM TO EXIT RESISTANCE

The biggest challenge with flamboyant teams when it comes to overcoming their unique resistance behaviors is their tendency to rush to action.

In order to sufficiently reinforce new synaptic pathways and replace the old ones as the new default response, strategies or synaptic pathways need to be accurately defined and sufficiently reinforced.

I have touched on the importance of accurate definition of new strategies in earlier chapters. As you'll see in Part Three, the way strategies are designed is critical for them to be effective and lead to desired outcomes. The greatest challenge with flamboyant teams is that they are too impatient; they run forward too fast, missing the definition of the new strategies along the way. If that's not enough, even when the flamboyant team can accurately define new strategies, team members are too impatient to reinforce it sufficiently. Even before they start, they want the process to be already over.

This brings us back to the importance of having the team's manager lead the acquisition process. Unlike the emotional oscillator cluster, flamboyant teams have no issues with authority and will easily submit themselves to following guidance if it comes with authority attached to it. They will not respond as favorably if an expert, regardless of how qualified or successful, tries to enforce the process. In those cases flamboyant teams can respond a lot like the emotional oscillator team. They will become offensive and even abusive, using tactics like detachment or a sense of superiority to dismiss the importance of the process in comparison to everything else they have going on, and flamboyant teams always have a lot going on. It's easy to see why entering through that door doesn't typically lead to desired outcomes.

Samantha was a senior VP in a high-tech organization. Samantha's name was associated with highly energetic and engaging behaviors when it came to clients and colleagues but with demeaning behaviors when it came to her staff. Everyone on her staff feared her or wanted to avoid her company. *"You'll hear horror stories about how she treats her team. She will humiliate people, manipulate them, and there's really no way to access her with feedback without being shot down for it. With that said, Samantha does want to be coached and she has made the time for it in the past."* VP of HR, high-tech industry

Samantha has been coached several times. Perhaps the best way to describe how her sessions went is to think of the initial scenes from "The Sound of Music". The kids must have had more than a dozen nannies but all of them ran away because of the children's pranks. Samantha definitely made the time for coaching, but she didn't genuinely make room for it.

People who say they are open to be coached but are not genuinely interested in changing are the inspiration for this book.

Where coaching and training doesn't work, the system in this book provides an answer. It's specifically designed for people like Samantha and for teams who struggle with change like the five cluster examples in this book.

Samantha's behavioral and thinking patterns fit the flamboyant cluster perfectly. She would not and could not adopt new behavioral patterns before because she didn't have access to the prerequisite strategies that were at the heart of those new patterns.

The solution with Samantha was to use a model we call Extraordinary Mentoring™. It gives managers like Samantha the strategies they needed by getting them to guide their team to acquire those same strategies. Extraordinary Mentoring™ worked for this team because the team needed the same strategies Samantha needed. The reason this works is because the lack of the same Key Strategy was responsible for the things that frustrated the team about Samantha, and for the things that frustrated Samantha about the performances of the team. While this isn't always possible, this "shared DNA" allows us to get people like Samantha to acquire needed strategies by guiding her team to acquire them. This shared DNA makes the Extraordinary Mentoring™ model a perfect solution for situations in which managers are the most resistant individuals on the team. It's more common when teams work together for long periods of time but when it does appear in the assessment report, it allows us to support change agents to change even the most difficult leaders and managers in their organization.

Resistance comes up very quickly with flamboyant teams. It comes in the form of delays and excuses for not delivering and following up. Flamboyant teams spend their time doing many tasks simultaneously, so getting them to focus on any single task may prove difficult. It's imperative to make sure the task is small enough, and then it's crucial to give clear instructions and set very clear, tangible goals and dates.

It's not a good idea to leave the early stages of goal forming and follow up to flamboyant teams. This does help pleasing teams to exit resistance by letting them set their own goals and pushing them to make choices, but it backfires with flamboyant teams. This is a great example for why understanding which strategies are missing for each team makes a huge difference. While the pleasing team will avoid initiative, the flamboyant team will almost abuse initiative.

When left to define the goals, flamboyant individuals and teams will talk their way right out of such a commitment or will define very vague and confusing goals. If you are managing a flamboyant team, come prepared, have tasks, goals and schedules well defined in advance. Don't forget to set a follow up meeting.

It's most likely that flamboyant teams will not complete the tasks you have assigned them in the time assigned. But with all their impatience and dislike of direction, flamboyant teams respond well to very clear boundaries with clear dates that come with authority. In the next meeting, ask them to bring up anything that may get in their way of completing the small task that was originally assigned. Make sure all questions are answered and get a firm commitment from the team that they will meet their goal this time around. Again, don't forget to set up a follow-up meeting. In our experience, these two steps, provided they are managed correctly, are usually enough for flamboyant teams to exit resistance and continue on to acquire needed strategies and desired outcomes in a sustainable way.

For Samantha, working with her team, guiding them to acquire the needed strategies while acquiring it herself, made a huge difference for everyone. It helped that the process was in no way remedial because, as we mentioned, flamboyant teams don't do well with being corrected. Samantha wasn't, at any point, asked to admit anything about her was broken, only that both she and her team needed to acquire new strategies in order for her to gain what she wanted and for the organization to benefit from better desired outcomes. It allowed for a natural win-win: Samantha got better results, letting go of her frustrations with the team's deliverables, and the team got to have a manager that could finally listen.

"After four weeks Samantha certainly had a breakthrough… She is still a very intense manager, but watching Samantha change was truly amazing. She resisted every step of the way initially… at some point she must have seen this as a good opportunity… she suddenly dropped her guard and I can see she is both more effective and more relaxed. I couldn't be more impressed with the results. She is finally giving the team room to grow and the team is now stepping up, which is what she wanted all along." VP of HR, high-tech industry

It's common to see a single individual like Samantha dictate the dynamics in a team. In most cases, the ways in which teams react, learn, plan, interact, and execute will lead to desired outcomes only if the influential individuals and their teams change. It's imperative to look at the team as a whole in those cases, in those cases, so that the system as a whole is balanced and that the manager and the team are equipped to continue holding the flamboyant individual accountable after the process is complete.

DO YOU KNOW A FLAMBOYANT TEAM, INDIVIDUAL OR ORGANIZATION?

Flamboyant teams:

★ Warm and highly socially skilled

★ Bring great energy to the interaction with team members and clients

★ Decisions and performances lack attention to detail and consistency

★ In planning and problem solving, will explore things widely but not deeply, will respond intuitively without checking many of the details

★ Prefer to have options and will create options if such are not abound

★ Will resolve conflict by directing all their attention to the problem. If the other side is equally understanding will try to have constructive win-win solutions. When that is not the case, they will either turn to hidden manipulations or will ignore the problem completely

★ Communication and team discussion style is uninhibited, people saying and doing whatever comes to mind

★ Are unable to postpone gratification, or withhold satisfaction, will often obsessively focus on what they want at the price of other urgent tasks

★ Will talk a great talk but deliver very little. When pressure around delivery increases, they depend even further on inspiration and more talk

GIVING FLAMBOYANT TEAMS ACCESS TO THEIR FULL POTENTIAL

Equip flamboyant teams with one to three of these strategies:

★ **STRATEGY #1**: Postponing Judgment: gives flamboyant teams the ability to slow down decision making process, forcing them to evaluate the reasoning and assumptions they are using before jumping to action. This strategy helps flamboyant teams moderate their need to explore new opportunities as well as see the part they play to contribute to the responses of others.

★ **STRATEGY #2**: Global Optimization Vs. Local Optimization: equips flamboyant teams with the ability to optimize globally or locally based on the task. This strategy is particularly important for flamboyant teams to further reinforce their ability to pay attention to detail, to slow down, and to align the detail of their local actions with the big picture.

★ **STRATEGY #3**: Systemic Thinking: flamboyant teams typically don't take into account how their actions will affect other people, areas and functions in the system. This strategy allows them to create higher coordination, accept the need to make room for other talents that compliment their own.

Additional highlights:

★ It's important to have the team's manager lead the acquisition process. Flamboyant teams have no issues with authority and will easily submit themselves to following guidance if it comes with authority attached to it.

★ It's imperative to make sure the task is small enough and then it's crucial to give clear instructions and set very clear, tangible goals and dates.

STABILITY TEAMS

"NOTHING IS WHAT IT SEEMS."

Excellence in execution is one of the most important outcomes to CEOs. The general idea is that teams should see a need, make choices about what to do or not do, and then execute, engaging in an ongoing methodical feedback loop until the needs have been fulfilled with excellence.

If reality in business were so predictable and linear, stability teams would excel every time. Unfortunately, excelling and executing are both much more complex and dynamic.

As you'll soon see, stability teams will do very well with any part of planning, structuring, or linear development that goes into execution. They will be great at creating clarity and focus, following the outlined path, evaluating and assessing and anticipating problems, often well in advance to allow appropriate, well thought out responses. But they will lack the ability to deal with the unexpected and the unknown. They will be slow to respond to new opportunities and will be in complete turmoil in the face of urgent changes that are forced on the system.

Of the five clusters in this book, the stability team is most focused on avoiding change. These teams don't enjoy unplanned or unexpected changes wherever they are. Typically the biggest change stability teams need is developing agility.

Donna was the VP of HR of a medium size company in the services industry. She has been in the company for seven years and worked closely with her CEO to build a new meaning for her role. Unlike her positions in the past where her role was limited to tactical HR tasks like overseeing compensation or training and development, she was able to contribute on the strategic level. *"Our goal this year is to align our efforts with our strategy and to create clarity. The feedback we get indicates that our leadership believes some of our goals contradict and that there isn't sufficient execution of communicated strategies. This year we have decided to take on the changes needed and focus on alignment in execution."* VP of HR, services industry

Teams in Donna's organization worked hard, were motivated and loyal. Goals were communicated effectively, there were excellent systems and procedures in place and teams followed those procedures. However, the company was blocked from reaching its predicted profit growth. The assessment revealed that people in the organization knew what the goals were but felt some of the procedures and guidelines didn't match with achieving those goals. It also revealed that when in question, people preferred to stick to the outlined procedures, not to the organizational goals.

What people believe in is often different than what people actually practice. Our focus is on results, on execution, and on implementation, and hence the focus is always on what the context of the team is in practice.

Stability teams are responsive and preventive trouble-shooters. They will easily adopt new regulations and will typically become somewhat obsessive about following instructions, because it gives them a sense of stability. These teams prefer for everything to be structured, planned out and, understood in advance before acting on it. Stability teams like sticking to old patterns so much that even if they fully see how a solution will achieve a desired result, they will be resistant to moving forward.

The strategies that showed up for Donna's organization were the strategies associated with the stability cluster. These teams feel most comfortable when systems and procedures are well-defined. In fact, structures and procedures are so important to them that they typically no longer focus on the big picture. Once procedures are defined, stability teams will need someone else to come in and make changes to those procedures. The way they do things becomes their comfort zone. It would be exhausting for them to constantly evaluate if what they are doing is aligned with goals.

It's not so much that stability teams don't know what the goals are. They typically have well defined strategic goals and an engaged workforce. It's more that there's a breakdown between the bigger picture and every day focus. The need to focus on the little things, to focus on structure, and to create stability and predictability get in the way.

The hallmark of these teams is fear, suspicion, and caution. They constantly expect things to go wrong. They will avoid confident statements and will diminish their successes because of the undesirable things they are concerned may still come.

Innovation for stability teams is nothing like the spontaneous, intuitive innovation of pleasing teams or flamboyant teams, for example. Despite the fact that all three clusters have great imaginative minds, the innovation of stability teams will be more around improvements to tried and sure processes than the out of the box, new thinking innovation of the pleasing cluster or the flamboyant cluster. Decisions will often be made with great hesitancy and insecurity because this cluster feels like there are many things still out there that they don't know enough about.

Like the other four clusters presented in Part Two, stability teams are missing very specific Key Strategies, thus blocking them from reaching their full potential. Without those strategies, trying to instruct these teams to align efforts with goals and to use guidelines to serve the goals, will most frequently not yield any improvement. Stability teams respond a certain way because they have a dependency on structure. To have the needed flexibility, these teams first must grow out of this dependency. To do that, you first need to guide them to establish new synaptic pathways in their brain.

Donna defined middle management as the most influential management layer for this transformation. Twelve managers were selected to guide their teams through five stages of acquiring needed strategies. Managers had to first adopt the new strategies themselves. It's not a requirement for the success of the change to involve senior leadership at the beginning of the process, but Donna elected to involve senior leadership from the onset, having the CEO guide the group of managers through the acquisition of the new strategies.

"What makes this solution unique is that it's less talking about the problem or defining the solution and more putting the new solution into action almost from day one. Even though we were invested in the results before, this is the first time we have seen clear unmistakable changes in results. The process was demanding initially, mainly because we were getting in our own way but I could not have asked for better partners to hold our hand as we achieved the results we set out to achieve. It's a transformational process, one that I highly recommend on every level." VP of HR, services industry

People often can't align their efforts with the business's strategy because they need to first acquire certain Key Strategies. Equipping teams with the right prerequisite strategies in a way that forms new default synaptic pathways allows teams to access their full potential.

THE STRATEGIES NEEDED TO SUPPORT THE STABILITY TEAM

Stability teams don't respond well to quick changes or to changes in schedule, load or goals regardless of how minor those are. Unplanned or unexpected additions such as new requests trigger instant resistance.

Renee was the Executive Director of a large nonprofit organization. The organization was growing rapidly attracting new board members who provided the organization with great new opportunities. *"Each time I bring up the new opportunities with the administrative team who will need to produce the events, I get pushed back. By their response you would think I'm giving them really bad news, when in fact this is the most exciting time for our organization in years."* Executive Director, nonprofit industry

All the team heard when Renee shared exciting new projects with them was the many adjustments they would have to make. This is a typical stability cluster response, one that in some cases indicates three very specific strategies are needed.

The three Key Strategies that allow stability teams to optimize productivity, giving them access to their potential are:

→ Conditioning to Questions and Separating Facts from Assumptions
→ Introspection and Emotional Articulation (around self-doubt and fears)
→ Deliberate Proactive Choice

STRATEGY #1: CONDITIONING TO QUESTIONS AND SEPARATING FACTS FROM ASSUMPTIONS

Stability teams confuse their own assumptions as facts. They often draw faulty conclusions about reality because they don't ask enough questions. But at the same time, they are very confident about their points of view or theories. Conditioning to Questions and Separating Facts from Assumptions makes it possible for these teams to further explore their blind areas and reach better conclusions.

Stability teams will often leave meetings with each member on the team understanding tasks differently or with decisions that don't take into account the needed considerations. Sometimes critical knowledge isn't integrated into solutions but team members don't challenge the decision or contribute that knowledge to the group because they assume the group already knows what they know.

It's common for stability teams to expect other people to know what they're thinking, which makes the communication style in this team full of miscommunications that are never exposed.

On Renee's team, people assumed the current overload they were experiencing could not be avoided or improved. They didn't think through what could be done. Instead they quickly drew a conclusion, based on fractions of reality and then avoided questioning them.

STRATEGY #2: INTROSPECTION AND EMOTIONAL ARTICULATION

Self-doubt is a very strong motivator for stability teams, and it holds them back from being active and proactive. Unfortunately, stability teams are not aware of the disabling thoughts that infiltrate their decision making process. They perceive themselves as highly logical decision makers, but fear and self-doubt block them from executing effectively.

They believe they're missing information.

It's futile to talk logic to stability teams and explain why they need to make decisions even when information is missing, or to ask them to act faster. Stability teams are unaware of their own barriers. This Key Strategy gives them access to those doubts and stoppers, allowing them to negotiate a better solution when in doubt.

Introspection and Emotional Articulation does not "heal" stability teams from having doubts. It does, however, give them a way to engage with those doubts by surfacing them and effectively responding to them.

Renee's team was completely consumed with self-doubt. Team members didn't believe they could achieve more than they already were. They didn't believe they would be able to take on more projects, and mostly, they feared the impact of what they didn't know, the additional hidden tasks that would go with the new projects.

STRATEGY #3: DELIBERATE PROACTIVE CHOICE

The Proactive Choice strategy gives people the ability to adopt an internal center of control instead of an external one. Stability teams believe things are happening to them. They don't take initiative because, among other things, they don't see what they could possibly do to improve the way things are.

In Renee's team, this created a very passive and reactive team that could not figure out how to do things differently. Though stability teams are excellent critics of what others need to change, and what problems exist in certain procedures or systems, they typically don't offer solutions. They will sometimes suggest superficial changes such as to do one task before another, but they won't come up with bigger picture solutions.

Asking Renee's team to be more flexible, without the

above strategies, would probably lead to very little progress. Stability teams don't want to change because they need certain new synaptic pathways.

Once the needed strategies were put in place, the team could approach new initiatives very differently than it did in the past. *"Before, each mention of change would lead to panic and to a long list of reasons outlining why it could not be done. Now it feels like the team can do anything. We shifted from a 'can't do' approach to a 'there's nothing we can't do' approach. This transformation is nothing short of a miracle."* Executive Director, nonprofit industry

When people who lack the strategies of the stability cluster are promoted to management positions, they can create stagnation in a team. The inaction of this cluster makes teams focus on bureaucracy or structural reasons as excuses for not making needed changes. You know exactly what I'm talking about if you've ever called a call service center and heard things like, "These are the policies" and "That's the regulation." The representative can't help you because they must follow the rules.

The need to accept things as they are and avoid any sudden or unplanned change makes stability teams rigid, hurting many critical business functions.

THE STABILITY TEAM BLOCKING DESIRED BUSINESS RESULTS

In most business sectors, agility is a critical defining factor of success. A 2009 organizational agility report by the Economist Intelligence Unit asked how business can survive and thrive in turbulent times. When asked about the critical traits of an agile organization, 61% of senior executives chose rapid decision-making and execution. Other important traits included high-performance culture, the ability to access the right information at the right time, accountability and credibility, and flexible management of teams and human resources among other things.

Not being able to rapidly make decisions makes it very difficult for stability teams to successfully compete.

Dennis was the executive director of a small startup that had been operating for several years in the biotech industry. The team wasn't making the progress Dennis was hoping for, but he just couldn't put his finger on what was off. *"We've had many opportunities that were lost. We know we offer great value because we have investors that are very committed to us. They believe, as do we, that the product is highly needed. It's mainly sales that we are worried about. We want to see more sales but we have no idea what we need to focus on. I wish there was a secret recipe book for this kind of stuff."* Executive Director, biotech industry

The assessment report for Dennis's team indicated a whole array of behaviors that matched the stability cluster. Most of the people on the team were extremely cautions, which slowed down the ability to respond to new opportunities. With new projects, team members often didn't follow up or take sufficient initiative to promote projects further. Team meetings were long. They set plans and clear steps that were followed meticulously, often at the price of responding to new opportunities. In addition, the team didn't use any systems to question bigger issues or to generate new thinking around improving. Dennis discussed the strategy of the company with colleagues and friends, but not so much with the team.

When change professionals talk about execution of change, they often discuss clarity of goals, transparency and effective communication. The assumption is that if people know what the organization needs to achieve, they will feel better connected to the goal and will be more engaged.

The reality in our experience is somewhat different. Clarity of goals works very well to motivate teams like the doubtful analyst or the pleasing team. However, when certain strategies are missing, like in the case of the stability team and the flamboyant team, clarity and communication cannot work without the foundation of certain needed strategies such as Postponing Judgment and Introspection and Emotional Articulation.

Stability teams are often blocked from optimizing their productivity and accessing their full potential because of these missing strategies.

Once the needed strategies were acquired by the team, the first sign of relief was that team members started to ask really good questions and design very valuable solutions. The very next thing that happened was they became proactive and resourceful. *"This process transformed the way our company operates. We were provided with a thorough analysis of the team's missing strategies which allowed us to be better tuned to the unique abilities we have and to the adjustments we needed to make. Of far greater importance, the process developed the essential mechanisms that maximized the potential of the staff's group dynamic and outcomes. The process made the individual work experience of each and every team member more satisfying but at the same time we changed and can now achieve desired results and alignment with our short term goals. I highly recommend this process. Try it, you won't be disappointed."* Executive Director, biotech industry

Not having certain strategies in place makes it difficult for stability teams to succeed in a complex, dynamic, or less predictable environment. It prevents companies from growing and puts them at high risk of being unable to compete in a fast-paced environment.

GUIDING THE STABILITY TEAM TO EXIT RESISTANCE

Unlike doubtful analyst teams and emotional oscillator teams, stability teams will not take offense at requests to improve. Provided the request is made with respect and in a predictable manner, stability teams take feedback gracefully. They understand nothing is perfect and they expect they are probably making mistakes along the way. Most of the time they don't see improvement requests as a personal issue.

If pushed or stressed however, stability teams will become extremely anxious and will focus on blaming others or everything else in the environment that, in their perception, is making it impossible for them to meet the requirements in the past and future.

This resistance is relatively easy to overcome. Simply set very clear goals, explain which changes are needed, and give stability teams time to process and get back to you with a plan and a schedule. As long as you are not surprising this cluster with something unexpected or unpredictable, you will typically find them extremely cooperative and willing to change.

The challenge with stability teams starts when you need changes to happen faster and you cannot afford for adjustments to happen on a slower schedule.

The first thing you'll need in order to accelerate change in these cases surrounds the exact definitions of what needs to change.

Stability teams will hear you make a statement but interpret it under their previous understanding. You may give the stability team very clear instructions and find they will not follow time and time again.

A good way to imagine this is to think of asking someone to present a point in a positive tone. You can tell them to focus on what they do want instead of focusing on what they don't want. You can ask them to offer a solution, use positive words or show them specifically why the way they phrase a sentence is negative. But despite all of that, stability teams will construct a negative statement and will be completely bewildered by why you think they are not doing as you asked.

It's their interpretation of definitions and of reality that gets in their way. Working with stability teams on the definitions of strategies will expose the differences to anyone observing, but not to stability teams themselves.

Jonathan was a team leader in a large organization. Marcus, one of the scientists on Jonathan's team was hoping to get promoted but Jonathan didn't feel Marcus could advance before developing certain "people skills." Marcus tried hard to apply the feedback Jonathan shared with him in the past, but it worried Jonathan that Marcus still didn't understand what was missing.

"Marcus is a great guy and I have a lot of respect for him. He is disciplined and he works really well within the team. His hope is to manage projects but I see him having a really hard time interacting with clients and managing others. We have had many conversations about this but even last week when I asked him to engage other team members to complete a simple task, he didn't get to it...I can't promote him in good faith until he improves these abilities." Manager, high-tech industry

According to Jonathan, Marcus always truly listened and agreed with Jonathan's explanations and expectations after a lengthy conversation. Still, the same situations came up over and over again. Marcus was driven but seemed to have too little initiative. He just didn't seem aligned with the expectations Jonathan expressed. Then the head of HR informed Jonathan that they are planning on offering a management development program in which Jonathan would be able to mentor one of the potential team members on in his team. Jonathan saw mentoring Marcus as a great opportunity.

Defining expectations with stability teams often feels like speaking with someone who hears your words but uses a completely different code to understand them. The effect is frustrating: you may be saying the same thing over and over again, and people who need the strategies of the stability cluster will claim they understand every word, but when you say green they'll hear red. You can ask stability teams to do something, they will believe they did exactly what you asked, but their actions will not be aligned with your expectations, proving they don't truly hear you.

Marcus' early definitions of the first strategy he needed to reinforce were most interesting. They were all examples about suffering and death and the suffering of people who had to deal with death. The theme of the new strategy was there but a stronger pattern was there too. He was repeatedly asked to give examples that created more topical variety, but his morbid examples continued.

The topic that stability teams or individuals stick to varies of course, but it's very typical for this cluster to be trapped in an invisible pattern. They don't see that they're trapped, and it's extremely difficult to show them without the right system in place.

The most important step required in order to get stability teams past their resistance is to identify any pattern that may be projected into experience based examples. They need to create examples that meet the definition you are after, clean of the patterns they are clinging to.

Once Marcus' fixation on irrelevant patterns was removed, Marcus could clearly see the strategies that he needed to acquire. He proceeded to acquire them quickly and effortlessly. Once those strategies were acquired, Marcus was finally able to let go of his hesitancies, become more proactive and access his potential. *"I have always believed in*

Marcus' abilities as a person but when it came to his growth I was genuinely concerned. This process gave Marcus an opportunity to do so much more than either one of us believed he would. Marcus and I still have conversations about things he needs to pay attention to, but his ability to initiate has improved in a meaningful way." Manager, high-tech industry

Stability teams resist because they're not able to create a new definition of what they see around them. While managers often think of resistance in terms of the specific responses people present, it's imperative to understand how and why different teams resist. If you don't know that stability teams resist because they have a hard time creating a new definition of reality, you may think it's their attitude, insecurity or pure stubbornness. Not knowing which strategy is blocking people in general makes managers respond to the wrong reasons and then assume it's people's personalities that are getting in the way.

The answer is having a system to identify which strategies are needed and how to get people to acquire them by reinforcing those new strategies as new default synaptic pathways in the brain. This can make the difference between having to deal with 90% of people who cannot and will not change or dealing with 90% of people who can easily adjust and make needed changes.

There are of course many other clusters and combinations of needed strategies that result in different team dynamics, different business outcomes and different resistances. Some are more emotionally based like the emotional oscillator cluster while some are more focused on the development of thinking skills.

Change the strategies people use and you will change their ability to adjust as well as your team's ability to achieve desired outcomes, optimize productivity and gain access to your business' full potential.

To do that requires two important things: identifying which Key Strategies will lead to desired outcomes and a system that will quickly allow people to acquire those new strategies.

DO YOU KNOW A STABILITY TEAM, INDIVIDUAL OR ORGANIZATION?

Stability teams:

★ Are excellent at problem solving and anticipating potential problems and critiquing plans to find possible threats

★ Are methodical, structured, and will easily adopt new regulations

★ Typically become somewhat obsessive about following instructions, because it gives them a sense of stability

★ Lack the ability to deal with the unexpected and the unknown

★ Will be slow to respond to new opportunities and will be in complete turmoil in the face of urgent changes that are forced on the system

★ Focus on the little things, on structure and on creating stability and predictability which sometimes gets in the way of focusing on the bigger goal

★ Are fear-based, suspicious, and cautious, constantly expecting things to go wrong

★ Will avoid confident statements and will diminish their successes because of the undesirable things they are concerned may still come

★ Will display innovation more around improvements to tried and sure processes

★ Become evasive, procrastinating, avoidant, or pretend like the stressor does not exist to regain their need for stability

★ Are anxious, focused on blaming others and on complaints as if everything else in the environment is making it impossible for them to meet requirements

★ Have difficulty making decisions, or indecisiveness as a result of self-doubt and fear

GIVING STABILITY TEAMS ACCESS TO THEIR FULL POTENTIAL

Equip stability teams with one to three of these strategies:

- ★ **STRATEGY #1**: Conditioning to Questions and Separating Facts from Assumptions: makes it possible for these teams to further explore their blind areas and reach better conclusions. This strategy helps stability teams avoid confusing their assumptions with facts, minimizing drawing faulty conclusions about reality and getting these teams in the habit of asking enough questions.

- ★ **STRATEGY #2**: Introspection and Emotional Articulation: stability teams are unaware of their own barriers, their own self-doubt and the effect these have on their ability to make decisions, take initiative and move their teams forward. This strategy allows stability teams to respond more effectively to fears, concerns, doubts, and other blocking barriers.

- ★ **STRATEGY #3**: Deliberate Proactive Choice: gives stability teams the ability to adopt an internal center of control instead of an external one. This further reinforces the ability to take initiative, respond faster to new situations and build flexibility and agility through a sense of having the ability to influence the world around them.

Additional highlights:

★ As long as you are not surprising this cluster by something unexpected or unpredictable, you will typically find them extremely cooperative and willing to change.

★ The most important thing required in order to get stability teams past their resistance is to identify any pattern that may be projected into experience based examples and keep insisting on them creating examples that meet the definition you are after, clean of the patterns they are clinging to.

PART THREE
A NEW SCIENTIFIC SOLUTION

People don't apply needed adjustments in a lasting way for a variety of different reasons. Some don't because they feel forced while others may be highly motivated and still not apply the agreed upon changes.

Perhaps the most important thing we want to share with you is that, in our experience, 90% of people who don't want to change don't because they can't. Even some of the most willing teams will not reach desired outcomes because they don't have access to strategies that will actually work. They also don't have access to a system that will lead to the acquisition of those new strategies.

When these two conditions are met, you'll discover that only approximately 10% of people truly make a choice not to apply needed adjustments. The rest, may initially resist but will quickly change, and make needed adjustments in a lasting way.

The solution starts with understanding the brain. Part Three covers three important areas of focus that contribute to this new system.

1. **THE IMPORTANCE OF DESIGNING STRATEGIES AS KEY STRATEGIES**: For the brain to prefer a new strategy over an old strategy, the strategies themselves need to be designed in a very particular way. Chapter Eight will explore the way in which key strategies are designed to make the brain prefer them as new default strategies.

2. **A NEW SYSTEM OF ACCELERATED ACQUISITION**: People make modifications to their synaptic pathways throughout their lifetimes but the speed and frequency of these will differ greatly from one person to another. The process of acquisition itself however, seems to be consistently the same. Knowing the stages people need to go through in order to acquire a new strategy or create a new synaptic pathway allows managers to accelerate the acquisition process from an unpredictable timeframe down to several weeks.

3. **THE NEW SCIENCE OF CHANGING PEOPLE**: Chapter Ten is a selected review of brain science research and the applications it has on changing people in general and especially on supporting people who can't or won't change. If you've ever been curious about the mechanisms that make people respond the way they do or why the solution presented in this book works, this is where you can find some of the answers. More about the scientific foundation for this book can be found online at: www. KeyChangeNow.com.

THE UNIQUE DESIGN OF KEY STRATEGIES

The key is to give people a "superior" strategy, meaning one that the brain will perceive as superior to other strategies.

Richard agreed to work with his R&D team mainly due to repeated pressure from manufacturing. As Systems Division Director in the telecom industry, he knew it was delaying other departments and frustrating clients when deadlines were not met. Richard's VP realized that development deadlines are not always in Richard's control but he wanted to explore a way to improve delivery issues. *"I understand there are creative aspects to R&D but I feel that somehow this is happening more frequently than it should. Richard is generally open to making any needed changes, it's just that we don't exactly know which kind of changes would help in this case."* VP of Engineering, telecommunications industry

It seemed like development was slowed down due to poor project management. Richard's team was made up of brilliant individuals. Why would such a capable team not adopt better project management habits? As the assessment of the situation deepened, it became very clear the problem wasn't that Richard and his team lacked the expertise to manage projects effectively. The real issue was that Richard and his team had good reasons, tracked back to the way their brains were wired, to insist on quality despite the prices of delays.

Richard believed the most important thing was for his team to keep very high accuracy standards. As an engineer, he felt things needed to be done in a certain sequence. He realized that sometimes when he pushed his team to improve standards before submission, that meant delaying production. He even knew that the sales department would be on his case. He was truly the only one who knew the prices of faulty R&D, and yet he believed it was better to delay production and avoid costly mistakes. Naturally, Richard's VP had a different perspective.

Getting someone like Richard to fully understand his VP's perspective, and the response required to balance production and sales, is not an intellectual exercise. You already know from reading about the five team clusters in Part Two that trying to convince someone like Richard to incorporate other perspectives can be a long and tedious process, and often a long battle of wits.

How do you get such a team to adopt other perspectives?

Over the years, working with many teams in a variety of industries, we have found there is a set of prerequisite strategies that together create highly effective teams. I have touched on some prerequisite Key Strategies such as KindExcellence™ and Synthesis vs. Analysis in Parts One and Two. When these strategies are missing, productivity will not be optimized and teams will not access their full potential.

Adding missing Key Strategies allows teams to make the needed changes and adjustments in order to achieve desired outcomes.

The assessment report found that Richard and his team were rigid about quality, without prioritizing other important business aspects because they needed Synthesis vs. Analysis, a Key Strategy I've mentioned in previous chapters.

For the purpose of understanding Synthesis vs. Analysis in this context, we can frame this strategy as the ability to shift from a decisive, determinate, "there is only one way" state of mind which is typical for people who have a high preference for analysis, to an open, flexible, inclusive state of mind. In extreme, people who are constantly in analysis mode tend to see things in black and white which made Richard, as well as his team, very rigid.

With the new strategy in place, Richard's team had access to seeing other perspectives. We didn't teach Richard's team how to listen, how to be less rigid or how to be more inclusive. The focus was to supplement Richard's team with the foundation of strategies the team needed in order to better listen, develop agility and be more inclusive. *"The first few weeks were concerning. We saw very little change and it seemed like this process, like the other approaches we used is about to fail. But then something really impressive happened, Richard's team transformed. It was like a strike of lightning. We have seen a complete shift in the team's approach to deadlines and to the priorities of other departments."* VP of Engineering, telecommunications industry

Key prerequisite strategies like Synthesis vs. Analysis create a platform that makes something that wasn't possible before possible. A good way to think about it is to imagine your team is ineffective presenting in meetings. You could explore and describe to your team the exact things that should be done in order to present effectively in meetings:

speak concisely, cover the main questions and action items, stay open to other comments and opinions etc. Each one of these is a description of effective performance but it doesn't give the team access to acquiring them. As I covered in Part One, an accurate description of effective performance doesn't support people in acquiring that performance. The description engages the Knowledge Based System and is stored as an accurate description, having very little effect on changes in outcomes. Without Key Strategies such as Synthesis vs. Analysis, teams don't have access to speaking concisely and without Key Strategies like KindExcellence™, teams don't have access to staying open to other opinions.

With the right strategies in place, teams can suddenly design the right systems and solutions all by themselves. Without it, no amount of practice in being more inclusive would have made a difference. With Synthesis vs. Analysis in place, there was no need to teach Richard's team to be less rigid.

TEAMS DON'T NEED TO AGREE THAT STRATEGIES ARE SUPERIOR IN ORDER FOR STRATEGIES TO LEAD TO DESIRED OUTCOMES

In 90% of cases, teams will need external support in order to try a new strategy consistently enough to give it a real chance. This is because most people's strategies are designed to keep people safe and change is associated with the unknown and with fear. In many cases, teams will do the first part of change unwillingly.

As you'll see in Chapters Nine and Ten, this initial unwillingness to genuinely commit to change or to acknowledge something is wrong doesn't get in the way of getting people to complete the process successfully.

In fact, as the title of the book indicates, our expertise is working with teams who initially don't make a genuine commitment to change, or are not willing to acknowledge they need to change. For a new strategy to be acquired, the brain doesn't need to agree the new strategies is superior up front, nor does it need to be convinced or agree with any logic. The only requirement is that the new strategy, after being sufficiently tested in practice, will prove to lead more consistently to success, without being limited to a specific situation or circumstance.

Think of trying to convince someone who is terrified of public speaking that there is nothing to fear and that they will do just fine. Talking and convincing won't get this person to change their mind about speaking. If, however, you could get that person to present enough times, with each time being perceived by that person as a success, that individual would end up enjoying speaking as a result, regardless of the initial strong response that individual had to speaking.

Initial resistance to change is inconsequential, and it can be totally ignored if you can get people to experience success practicing a new strategy. There is no need for initial long term commitment or for an upfront acknowledgement that a certain strategy is the right strategy. The test is simple: if people try the strategy, and in their perception it's better for them than old strategies, the brain will consider these strategies as superior to old strategies.

There is no need to make sure people see why a certain strategy is superior to older strategies in order for the brain to acquire the strategy. The superiority of a strategy is proven in practice, not through logic.

SOME STRATEGIES ARE PERCEIVED BY THE BRAIN AS SUPERIOR TO OTHERS

Why should the brain "agree" to replace the strategies it has been reinforcing for new strategies?

The brain doesn't treat all strategies equally. The more strategies prove to serve us well by our own perception, or the more they can prove valuable across different situations, the more our brain will want to keep these strategies.

Liz felt held back for the last three years. In her role as Director of HR and operations in a large agricultural company, she saw how the growth in sales had slowed down over the last few years and has been tracking productivity for a while. *"Our CEO has been in the company for five years and was able to establish new values and work ethics in this time. He is a natural leader and people have great respect for him. Despite his great leadership he feels stuck when it comes to our sales department. It seems like half of the time he has to talk about the importance of relationships in sales. He spends the other half dealing with client complaints. He would really rather focus his time on growing the company. Instead he often talks about feeling held back by his own people."* Director of HR and Operations, agricultural industry

Even their best agents didn't spend enough time on the phone. Their CEO often had to rush back to call clients because clients were outraged by the service they received and as the Director of HR and Operations, Liz felt there was more they could do to support the teams and the CEO.

The goal was to increase capital by focusing on greater outreach and business development, but in order to increase capital several things within the company needed to change. To create new resources, the CEO needed to free resources. He expected people to take more responsibility and more initiative. *"When you talk to managers and teams about what needs to change, people immediately look at what other departments should do differently. I'd like to see managers and teams take more responsibility for what they need to do."* CEO, agricultural industry

The team's perspective was that the organization was managed by a highly controlled and centric approach. Team members and middle management had great respect for the leadership team and the CEO in particular, but the management culture, as identified by the team, was one that led to dependency and lack of initiative.

Getting people to make needed adjustments and changes that will lead to desired results starts with pinpointing a Key Strategy, one that the brain will prefer over other strategies and when adopted will lead to desired outcomes.

In the case of Liz's organization, the desired result was that sales people would invest more time nurturing clients and that the service level would go up to minimize complaints. Leaders in the organization believed these two changes would free the CEO's time to further grow the company. A deeper assessment of which Key Strategy was missing highlighted a Key Strategy we call "Global Optimization vs. Local Optimization."

You have already met this strategy in Part Two as one of the Key Strategies needed for flamboyant teams to access their full potential. In essence, global optimization is the preference to optimize long term, system wide considerations while local optimization is a preference to optimize immediate concerns. Sometimes teams use local optimization or global optimization without considering which approach is a better fit for specific situations. Most of the time, the old invisible strategy that is blocking the team is a preference for one or the other. Choosing which approach will be a better fit for different situations is a strategy the brain will perceive to be superior to using either one of the above optimization approaches.

Aside for producing better perceived results in practice, strategies will be considered superior by the brain if they are designed to increase desired results. If you are practicing a strategy that directs you to withdraw each time someone speaks to you with authority, there is no learning or refinement going on. A strategy that will direct you to choose when to withdraw and when to hold your ground will teach you much more and will be more effective as a result.

Generally speaking, strategies that are set up like a simulator work better than strategies that are directive.

Pilots use a simulator to develop intuitive decisions through an experience based feedback loop. If the pilot chooses a wrong action, the plane may crash. Over time, using the simulator, pilots develop sensitivity to nuances, making it possible for them to intuitively make better experience-based decisions.

Key Strategies are much like developing an internal simulator. Learning to constantly examine which situations require prioritizing global optimization over local optimization and vice versa is an ongoing excellence mechanism. If Liz gave sales people clear instructions on when to use global optimization and when to use local optimization, she may have gotten higher productivity for simple tasks, but because the internal simulator would have been missing, the effectiveness of the team would still have been limited.

In the sales team, the need for this strategy took the shape of lack of initiative, delaying responses to clients and less than optimal prioritizing. In other places in the organization, the need for this strategy exhibited itself in other ways. Where senior management was concerned, for example, the highest priority was to solve problems, complaints and obstacles as quickly as possible, which often meant managers would storm in and take over. Without Global Optimization vs. Local Optimization, teams didn't prioritize effectively, stopped taking initiative, causing managers to take over. Managers did the same, allowing the organization's leadership to take over.

Any single one of these dynamics on their own could mean a million other things, but together they create a strong pattern that clearly indicates the need for Global Optimization vs. Local Optimization.

Designing strategies as simulators instead of using directive strategies has another advantage. Not only does this act as a self-reinforcing mechanism for excellence, it's also the missing foundation for acquiring many needed skills. Some strategies are superior because they are prerequisites for other things to work.

For Liz's team, pinpointing the needed strategy allowed the team to make needed adjustments. Not only did the sales team make needed changes, so did the CEO and other leaders in key positions. *"...the results are inspiring. The gap between middle management and senior management is bridged. People are taking initiative, taking responsibility for their own results and efforts. As we predicted, we are starting to see signs of increase in sales and reduced expenses. What's interesting is that now that our managers have learned how to get productivity up, the teams seem to have access to many of the tools we gave them in the past."* Director of HR and Operations, agricultural industry

Skills that are limited to certain tasks, such as practicing how to close a sale, or manage a project or a meeting, are great tools. They are the result of years of observation and refinement, and there is no need to reinvent the wheel every time we approach a new task. That said, no two sales are exactly the same, no two projects will run at the same speed and get stuck for the exactly same reasons, and no two meetings should be managed exactly the same. For teams to excell, people need to acquire strategies that can apply nuanced learning, not just mimicking and repeating a set of processed, broken-down observations made by other people.

WHY DO SOME STRATEGIES LEAD TO BETTER RESULTS THAN OTHERS?

The brain will only adopt new strategies if it perceives them to be better than old strategies. Perception is enough but it also helps if the strategies are actually designed to lead to better results.

As the HR Director in a large defense corporation, Claire saw the response managers had to evaluation as an undesirable byproduct of an otherwise wonderful organizational culture. Not many large corporations could keep up with the strong connections managers had with their teams, especially in this industry. But looking at the bigger picture, Claire knew not all managers were the same and not all teams were promoted fairly. *"We would like to see the system we have for evaluation more adequately used. Right now, very few managers are using our structured evaluation process with their teams. We have no real criteria for employee development but managers are resisting a more formal process, saying that it is contrived and inefficient. They'd much rather just give promotion recommendations but on a strategic HR level we need standardization."* HR Director, defense industry

Claire understood that managers wanted to maintain an authentic relationship with their teams, but she felt she had to create a system that would work for the organization as a whole, not just for individual managers. The reasoning managers provided in the assessment was that they didn't want the new evaluation system to have a negative effect on the informal relationships they built with their teams. In their perception, there was only one way to use the evaluation process and it wasn't a good fit for their needs.

In meetings, managers expressed a great deal of resistance to adopting the new evaluation process. Their explanations seemed irrational, but managers were insisting on doing things a certain way without allowing the discussion to examine any other options. They didn't see Claire's point of view and she felt they were not really listening. It was as if they were trying to protect something, perhaps trying to avoid any changes, but changes needed to be made.

In this case, the main strategy needed was Conditioning to Questions and Separating Facts from Assumptions. I have touched on this strategy in Part Two when I discussed stability teams. This strategy helps people avoid treating assumptions like facts or treating facts like assumptions. When people mix these two, they can end up jumping to faulty conclusions, have limited perspective of possibilities, and develop a false certainty about things that need to be further explored.

Certain strategies work better than others because they have a wider effect on different situations and circumstances. A team that works under a strategy of "question everything," or a team that doesn't doubt its own thinking processes are both going to be less successful than a team that knows when to question things and when not to have doubts.

Similarly, a strategy that is limited only to certain situations will be considered less powerful than a strategy that applies to most or all situations. Specific strategies that recommend doubting in situations x, y, and z while being confident in situations a to d, will not be as strong as strategies that will give people the ability to distinguish between situations that require questioning and situations that require no doubt.

Key Strategies are more effective because they apply successfully to many more situations than other strategies.

The brain perceives these strategies as super strategies because they are. They always apply.

Without this strategy, Claire's team believed their point of view was the only point of view possible. It's not so much that they disagreed with the point of view of others, they didn't really hear or register those points of view in the first place. When this strategy is missing, problems will arise in a variety of areas. For these, the autopilot response of not questioning any assumptions was apparent during meetings with their teams, and in faulty decisions teams made that later could be traced back to faulty assumptions and more.

Once Claire could engage managers by interacting with them through this new strategy, managers could for the first time hear Claire and respond effectively. Not having access to this strategy made managers seem stubborn and unreasonable, but in reality they simply didn't have access to their own potential. They didn't respond effectively because they didn't hear or see a big part of what was going on around them.

"We appreciated the breakthroughs that allowed us to make a transition to a new evaluation process. It was really hard to get to our managers and make them see the value of the new system. This workshop really gave them the perspective they needed in order for them to make the evaluation process work with their own management style." HR Director, defense industry

While the right strategy can lead to great results, identifying which strategies will lead to desired outcomes can be confusing. The only way to know for sure which strategy is needed in order to optimize productivity in each situation, and reach desired outcomes, is to look at patterns in the team or in the organization.

The success of the process as a whole depends on a lock and key combination. If the right strategy isn't identified, the process will run its course, and teams will spend time learning great strategies that will create marginal benefits, but that will not lead to desired outcomes. Some combinations of strategies are more common than others, and we have already shared some of the more common ones, but each situation needs to be evaluated carefully, taking into account team patterns as well as defined goals. The job of our detailed assessment process is to pinpoint the right combination of strategies that will lead to desired results.

A missing needed strategy will leave traces in different situations and this also gives Key Strategies a huge advantage. When teams acquire a single Key Strategy, it optimizes many different aspects simultaneously.

STRATEGIES MUST BE ACQUIRED IN EVOLUTIONARY ORDER

Terry has been managing sales teams for over 25 years. As the Sales Director of a pharmaceuticals corporation, he had excellent sales people on his team that have been in sales for over 20 years themselves. The more experienced sales people working for him understood sales almost naturally. They were excellent in creating the right relationships with the right people, making sales seamless. The more junior sales people were more of a concern. It seemed to Terry that their insecurities made them present an all knowledgeable front that tampered with the relationships and with an effective sale.

"Perhaps more than anything my priority is for our new sales people to understand the importance of building relationships and keeping relationships rather than pushing products...it wouldn't hurt them to be more open to learning from more experienced sales people and to do more consistent follow up. Our most successful sales people know the person they are speaking to, that doctor's or administrator's needs, they are confident because they have a good understanding of the product but with the client they don't go in as experts, they go in with curiosity and genuine interest to give our clients the best service possible." Sales Director, pharmaceutical industry

The assessment indicated that younger sales people were defensively insisting they could solve their own challenges while more experienced sales people expected that new sales representatives would have more curiosity about things that worked in the past and about their clients. Terry saw this lack of curiosity in conversations with clients. He felt junior sales people needed to learn to listen and to ask much better questions instead of focusing on features and benefits of one product over another.

Strategies serve different purposes, providing an answer to different hierarchical needs. When the lack of a certain strategies leads to dysfunctional or irrelevant emotional responses such as defensiveness, aggressiveness, or avoidance, there will often be more than one strategy needed.

The first strategy will need to provide a foundation that will eliminate dysfunctional responses. Generally speaking, emotional based strategies such as Postponing Judgment or Introspection and Emotional Articulation must be established before strictly thinking related strategies like Global Optimization vs. Local Optimization or Synthesis vs. Analysis.

As people develop strategies throughout their lives, they fall into response patterns triggered by not getting what they want or getting what they don't want. People respond with anger outbursts, silence, avoidance and a whole spectrum of behaviors, often in a certain sequence in order to deal with the consequences on an unmet need. In other words, the need is real, but as a result of experience-based learning, people develop strategies that are less than optimal.

People who don't know how to effectively gain control, for example, may be domineering, submissive, or dismissive, depending on the strategies they live by. Insecurities can lead to defensiveness; fear may lead to passive responses.

While the same team may also need strategies that are more evolutionarily "advanced," it will be impossible for them to acquire those until the emotionally-based strategies are supplemented. In a way, effective emotion-based strategies block access to advanced strategies and to optimizing productivity in general.

While 90% of people don't want to change or seem to be unable to change, teams who need an emotionally based strategy will often feel much more resistant and difficult.

Teams vary and the same symptom can, in different teams, be a result of not having access to different effective strategies. Not wanting to accept help or advice from more experienced sales people can be a result of missing strategies related to control, self confidence, an inability to see more than one option and many other possible strategies. As mentioned earlier, the only way to identify which specific Key Strategies will optimize productivity and give the team access to their full potential is by looking at the patterns in the team.

In this case, the strategy that led to desired outcomes was Postponing Judgment. This strategy, like most emotionally-based strategies, has many faces but it basically provides a buffer between decision and action.

When new sales people on the team were introduced to new things, they instantly wanted to go to a confident place and express their knowledge. Once the new strategy was in place, the defensive behavior stopped completely, in a lasting way. The new strategy allowed the team to build a culture of learning and cooperation and new sales people quickly acquired inquisitive and caring behaviors with clients.

"What I have noticed is that sales people are now much more natural around clients. I see them much more receptive, asking for advice and sharing problems much more freely with more senior sales people on the team. It used to be that if anyone offered them feedback they would find some excuse to cut the conversation short. Now they really listen and they listen to clients too. We are seeing clear improvement of sales ratios. The

program has accelerated their learning curve." Sales Director, pharmaceutical industry

When working with people who you consider difficult or people who first need emotionally-based strategies, I'd like to offer an important word of warning.

Sometimes when an environment is stuck, people may develop highly resistant or otherwise difficult behaviors, and it's not because they are lacking the necessary effective strategy. Sometimes highly effective people may turn difficult because their interaction with their environment doesn't allow them to apply effective strategies.

Just because a group of managers doesn't cooperate with a new system or make changes to meet a certain need doesn't necessarily mean managers are making the wrong decision or responding in an irrelevant or less than optimal way.

Sometimes, quite often actually, teams don't want to cooperate with change because the way the change is designed doesn't serve them in an optimal way. Their resistance exposes a certain lack of alignment or an important gap that needs to be addressed. Sometimes no one stops to listen to what these managers know. They are ignored. The best answer is to make sure you have designed the solution correctly, separating resistance that should make you rethink your solutions from resistance that comes from missing Key Strategies, taking into account the whole complexity of the challenge at hand. When you have, you'll be able to bring on board even the most stubborn and difficult people 90% of the time.

OTHER CONSIDERATIONS FOR THE WAY EFFECTIVE STRATEGIES ARE DESIGNED

When you want people to make needed adjustments in order to increase productivity, effectively respond to strategic initiative, or otherwise access your organization's potential, it's important to align what you do with the way the brain changes.

The brain naturally builds strategies throughout people's lifetimes in a very specific way. When strategies are already formed, it becomes more difficult to change them because people start seeing everything through the lens of these strategies. Once we see the world through certain lenses, everything fits and can be explained through these lenses. This is such a powerful phenomenon that, if you don't have access to the right way to change people, you'll sometimes repeat a statement ten times, and though people tell you they understood, their actions will indicate otherwise. Jonathan's experience with Marcus's morbid examples, discussed in Chapter Seven, is a great illustration of that phenomenon.

To change people, it's important to switch people from this autopilot mode to a state of deliberate initiation. Because of the way the brain works, as long as people follow you, mimic you or in any way opt out of initiating their own choices, new strategies will not be formed and people will not change in a lasting way.

It's imperative that strategies are designed in a way that takes into account as many considerations as possible when it comes to how the brain can acquire them and turn them into application.

Steven was the Executive VP of Regional Innovation for a large telecommunications corporation. The way Steven saw it, innovation was a cultural foundation for his organization, not just a creative effort that was related to a specific project or problem. *"Our goals for the process we are building in the organization are to minimize the rejection of new ideas and increase focus on applicability. The assessment clarified two main areas that I believe in deeply: that we want to avoid situations in which managers and teams reject and diminish combination of ideas from different sources and that we need a more inclusive approach and follow through. There is often a sense of pessimism toward new ideas or approaches, teams giving up easily and not sufficient follow through on ideas that could be developed in a meaningful way."* Executive VP of Regional Innovation, telecommunications industry

Steven believed that teams were too quick to dismiss new ideas, that they often wanted to invest in a purist way instead of trying to combine older ideas. He thought they were often lacking focus, and were becoming too fascinated with the process instead of focusing on the purpose at hand. He believed it wasn't a skills issue but that these aspects were directly related to the organizational culture. The assessment highlighted that teams perceived good experiments were frequently abandoned because they failed, without recognizing them for the learning value they had. Managers felt teams had a general pessimistic attitude toward new ideas or approaches and that employees often assigned responsibility for the leadership of projects to their managers instead of taking more initiative.

In looking at a variety of different perspectives, patterns and symptoms in this organization, the strategy that tied up all the ends was one we have run into before, Synthesis vs. Analysis. Teams that use this strategy can quickly switch between an open, exploratory mode of discovery and an analytical, linear, organized approach on and off throughout a project. These two thinking states are so different that the brain uses different wave lengths to perform analysis than it uses to perform synthesis. When in analysis, the brain is discriminatory, judgmental, linear, and literal. This means that if teams are applying analysis when they need to be open and creative, the result will be teams that are too quick to dismiss new ideas or judgmental interactions that doom good ideas and do not foster exploration. At the same time applying synthesis, open flow, and a more relaxed approach to tasks like follow up and project management leads to lack of focus, efficiency and effective follow up.

Technically, Synthesis vs. Analysis could have been designed as a skill. We could have identified which situations call for synthesis and which call for analysis, and had people practice each. Instead, Key Strategies are designed to make people choose on an ongoing basis in order to increase the initiation requirement for creating new strategies in the brain.

We have already discussed the importance of designing most Key Strategies as simulators rather than as directive rules. There is one more reason why making a choice is so critical for engaging with the right system in the brain: the EBS will only encode a new strategy from experience if people initiate that experience. Interestingly, people can encode a new strategy based on someone else's experience as their own, but they will not encode a strategy, even based on their own experience unless it was initiated by them.

Think of a boy watching his sister being bit by a dog. The boy sees his sister's response, and as a result, the boy subconsciously concludes dogs are dangerous and unpredictable and that he shouldn't get close to dogs. Someone else's experience can form strategies that will affect people's behavior.

Imagine however that the girl didn't perceive the bite as a big deal. Maybe her mother or brother react by telling her to be careful and that dogs are dangerous. She will register in her KBS that her mother and brother believe dogs are dangerous, and she will probably remember being bitten. That said, the rules other people shared with the girl about her own experience will not be encoded in the EBS unless the girl initiates those conclusions herself.

Because of the way the brain works, Key Strategies need

to be initiated consistently by the people who need to change and they must be directly linked to practice.

The superiority of Key Strategies is that, because of their simulator design, they require an initiation of choice each time they are being practiced.

The only way to truly understand a strategy like Synthesis vs. Analysis is to apply it to a variety of situations. Strategies do not stand on their own, and they are not something we can learn from listening to someone talk about them or watch someone perform them.

If practiced correctly, however, Key Strategies can be acquired in a brief time, translating into action in a consistent way from that moment on and for the rest of people's lives. Initially using the strategy and making the choices prescribed by the strategies requires a deliberate effort for a few minutes a day. In a few weeks, the brain makes the choice in a split second and the strategy is activated deliberately, and often away from the team's awareness.

The beauty in this is that when the strategy is designed correctly it continuously forces people to initiate choice. This makes people continue to reinforce the strategy without having to invest any additional conscious effort.

For Steven's team, practicing Synthesis vs. Analysis was transformational. *"The program was exciting and it was wonderful to discover something we can easily do differently to increase innovation which is one of our organizational goals. Managers have changed their approach and are much more tolerating of thought-through failure and there is much more goal driven experimentation going on. Overall it has been a great success."* Executive VP of Regional Innovation, telecomm industry

Thinking of people who don't want to change in terms of Key Strategies redefines the solutions we offer organizations.

There are many excellent resources out there outlining which culture should be adopted during a merger for example. Putting those cultures in terms of Key Strategies gives us insight into how to get a particular team to adopt that new culture. When you run into excellent tools for sales, leadership, and communication, adding the perspective of Key Strategies makes it possible to pinpoint which strategies will get those skills acquired and applied quickly and in a lasting way.

The way teams act, make decisions, solve problems, interact, and innovate are all representations of the strategies people are using. Get people to change those strategies in a lasting way and you'll have changed all of the above.

Equally important is that teams resist change in accordance with the strategies they have at the time. This means that teams who need Global Optimization vs. Local Optimization may resist by believing they don't have time to invest in anything that isn't urgent. Teams who are lacking Postponing Judgment may be too impatient, constantly trying to rush to action instead. People who need Synthesis vs. Analysis may believe they know best and have no tolerance for opinions that contradict their own. Simply put, looking at changing people who don't want to change through the perspective of Key Strategies colors resistance in the shades of the strategy that is missing.

This is important because then resistance becomes predictable and relatively easy to manage.

Finally, as much as it's important for strategies to be designed correctly and actually lead to better results, strategies cannot stand alone.

Recognizing a new strategy as superior doesn't by any means guarantee that people will adopt that strategy. In fact, as I have already indicated, in 90% of cases even superior strategies will not be acquired without the right system.

Two things need to happen simultaneously. The strategies should be the right strategies, but they need to be combined with the right system, delivered in the right environment, in order for the brain to acquire them in a lasting way. The brain can quickly adopt Key Strategies if they are combined with the right acquisition system.

CHAPTER 8:
TAKEAWAYS

★ There is a set of prerequisite strategies that together make up a sort of "DNA" for highly effective teams.

★ It's imperative that strategies are designed in a way that takes into account as many considerations as possible of how the brain can acquire them and turn them into applications.

★ 90% of people who don't want to change initially, will change if they are willing to let someone else hold them accountable for using a new strategy that then proves to be better in practice.

★ Recognizing a new strategy as superior doesn't by any means guarantee that people will adopt that strategy. In fact, in 90% of cases even if strategies are perceived as superior they will not be acquired without the right acquisition system.

★ Generally speaking, strategies that are set up like a simulator work better than strategies that are directive.

★ When a needed strategy is missing it will have traces in different places, around different functions, blocking the organization from achieving its goals in a variety of ways, these can be identified as patterns and give insight into which strategies are needed.

★ When one Key Strategy is acquired it optimizes many different aspects simultaneously.

★ Typically, emotional-based strategies must be established before strictly thinking-related strategies.

A NEW SOLUTION

Incorporating the ability to change people into business solutions makes it possible to achieve desired outcomes 90% of the time.

Until about ten years ago, scientists didn't have the conditions and equipment needed in order to study the systems in the brain related to change. In the absence of seeing into the world of synaptic activity, change and development theories had to depend solely on observation. Since people seemed to stop changing after a certain age, it was believed the brain can no longer change, personality is fixed, change is associated with pain, and other such misconceptions.

Thanks to advances in brain science, we can now design solutions that affect people to make the adjustments needed in order to achieve desired outcomes.

There are numerous studies that cover the top ten challenges CEOs define for their companies. Though results vary for different industries and different countries, some focus areas consistently come up, such as:

→ Consistent execution of strategy
→ Stimulating innovation and differentiation
→ Speed, flexibility, and adaptability to change
→ Profit growth
→ Creating long-term value
→ Self-renewal and re-invention

Of course, if teams are to achieve these focus areas, people are not the only contributing factor for success, but the ways people learn, plan, interact, and execute are certainly important components to consider. It's probably the single most important variable for making a quantum leap in results.

We have found that whichever goals your organization has for the coming year, those goals most likely require people to make certain adjustments.

→ Which changes are needed in order for your organization to achieve your goals?
→ Which adjustments do people need to make in how they learn, plan, interact, and execute in order for teams to make the needed business changes and achieve their desired outcomes?
→ Which prerequisite strategies are required in order for teams in your organization to make these needed adjustments?

This new solution offers teams access to making the needed adjustments quickly and seamlessly by gifting people the needed platform to achieve those adjustments.

Some teams are already aware of most or all of the adjustments needed in order to achieve desired outcomes. In other cases some of those are still not clear or there is disagreement around needed adjustments. In those cases, the first order of business is to prepare the team to identify on its own which adjustments would lead to desired results.

As you've seen throughout the book, sometimes strategies are needed in order for the team to establish the right decisions about the team's direction or to identify which specific adjustments need to be made to achieve desired outcomes. In other cases the team is already in agreement and it seeks to execute at a higher level. In all cases, as I discussed, it's first imperative to identify which Key Strategies if put in place, will allow the team to make needed adjustments and achieve desired outcomes in a lasting way.

Each team and each organization is different. As you saw in Part Two, the specific set of strategies that will benefit your team will most likely be different than those of other organizations, even if they are trying to achieve the same goals you are trying to achieve.

In our work with organizations, creating clarity around the needed strategies is always the first step, but of course it then must be combined with a process that guides teams to acquisition and application. Once we have mapped which strategies will lead to desired outcomes it's time to treat change as if 90% of people in your organization need a foundation in order to make needed adjustments. It's then time to focus on supporting you in achieving your goals by focusing on the 90% of people who cannot or will not change.

The solution offered in this chapter brings together everything I have discussed throughout the book. If applied correctly, the solution works without the understanding of why it works. It helps, of course, to give managers the background of why things are designed the way they are, but managers don't need to first read a lengthy book in order to successfully change people.

It took years of observation, learning from our many mistakes and fine-tuning our successes to be able to present you with a coherent model for change. It's now a user-friendly toolkit that can be used by managers to facilitate desired results. Instead of exposing managers to the entire body of knowledge, the solution is tailored and the preparation pinpoints only what those managers need, specifically for their needed strategies, specifically for the goal they aim to achieve.

In refining this solution, we have noticed some things change from one team to another and from one organization to another, while other things stay consistently the same.

One of the things that stayed consistently the same, and is the topic of this chapter, was the steps people needed to follow in order to achieve lasting change.

As you'll see in Chapter Ten, the EBS is designed to allow people to adopt change throughout people's lives. It's designed to allow people to continue developing better, more refined rules about engaging with the world. However, most teams are not familiar with the process they need to go through in order to change. It seems like the 10% of people who can change in a lasting way on their own have somehow intuitively figured out how to quickly go through this process. They may not be aware of it, but they are following a very specific sequence.

It's a five-stage process, starting with a definition of desired outcomes, ending with lasting application of needed adjustments. These five stages are a representation of the natural learning process people apply when they acquire change through the EBS. It's a natural process for acquiring change through experience that people stop following for a variety of different reasons. It's the most empowering gift you can give teams: the ability to change themselves.

Most importantly for the purposes of this book, when managers can get teams through these five stages quickly and efficiently, taking into account everything we know about the science of changing people, teams make adjustments quickly and in a lasting way 90% of the time.

In Part One, we talked about a path leading up to a gate where, before changing people, felt like trying to break through an impassable boarder. Keeping on track with the five stages is the path. Skip a stage or stop progressing before you complete the process and you can expect to see lasting change in only 10% of cases. Guide people, even the most resistant and difficult people, through the process, and you'll find 90% of them making needed adjustments in a lasting way.

This chapter is about those five stages, about keeping your team on the path and about helping you build teams that can self-improve to access their full potential.

KCI'S FIVE-STAGE ACQUISITION SYSTEM

Throughout the book, we have explored many examples of team goals, organizational goals and individual goals that were achieved by focusing on changing the way people learn, plan, interact, and execute, especially when people were unwilling or unable to change.

I would like to invite you to define your own goals and explore how everything I discussed in this book can apply to giving your team access to higher productivity, to making needed adjustments, and to achieving your organization's priorities.

Take a moment to define desired outcomes for your organization, team or for an individual in a critical role in your organization:

....

....

....

....

Do you have a theory about which type of adjustments need to be made in the way people learn, plan, interact or execute that would lead to achieving the goals you have outlined? Write those down:

....

....

....

....

....

Which gain, fiscal or otherwise will the organization get if the adjustments will be made in a lasting way?

....

....

....

....

Who should be involved other than those who need to make the adjustments?

....

....

....

....

Will the people who need to change agree with the need for adjustments as you define them?

....

....

....

....

How do the people who need to change define the desired outcomes from their perspective? What do they complain about most? How will achieving the desired outcomes you defined from your perspective help them achieve their own goals or eliminate something that discomforts them? This one can be tricky but when Key Strategies are missing people are blocked in many ways. There always is a win-win, you just have to find it.

....

....

....

....

....

....

As I explore the system we developed over the years, please consider your desired outcomes and the people in your team that need to change. Think about their responses as if they were going through the different stages. What would their resistance look like? How flexible would they be to being introduced to new Key Strategies?

Unlike other solutions, this solution assumes people will initially not want to change. As we mentioned before, initial lack of cooperation is inconsequential. Our success is not conditioned by early cooperation. In fact, as you'll soon see, we expect resistance and typically assume it's there even if early behaviors indicate otherwise.

If you follow the system in this book, you can get even the most difficult people to make needed adjustments that will benefit them as much as it will benefit your organization.

The KCI system is a five-stage process that, in most cases, must be facilitated by a manager. The length of the process varies from team to team, but in most cases transformations are typically noticeable in a matter of weeks.

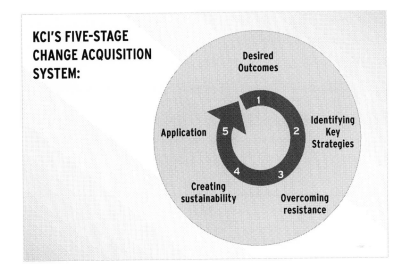

KCI'S FIVE-STAGE CHANGE ACQUISITION SYSTEM:

These five stages are the natural stages people need to go through in order to create a new synaptic pathway in the EBS in the brain. If you leave people to it, they will progress stage by stage until they complete the process on their own or until they get stuck. In most cases, you can expect the latter.

The climax of this system is the third stage: overcoming resistance. Note that sometimes, with pleasing clusters for example, it will be important to aggravate resistance. In those cases and for other considerations in other cases, it's beneficial to share the stages with each team at the onset of the process, until resistance has surfaced and is managed.

Knowing the five stages allows managers to accelerate the acquisition of needed strategies, instead of allowing people to go through the process at their own pace.

The five natural stages people go through must be sequential. People shouldn't move on to the next stage before they have completed the previous.

STAGE 1: DESIRED OUTCOMES

In order for people to change, people need to have a reason

to change that motivates them to invest time and energy in acquiring the change. Without a reason to change, people will not change or make needed adjustments in a lasting way.

Most change processes require that the motivation for change will come from agreement on the need for change. With other solutions, if you want your team to change the way they communicate, respond to a merger, or adopt new regulations or new technology, you first need your team to commit.

The system in this book challenges this misconception. With this system, you don't need to start with trust, and you don't need to start with agreement. You don't need people to acknowledge they need to improve and genuinely intend to apply the needed adjustments in order for the process to work.

The assumption here is that, at this point, teams don't want to change. Even if they are cooperating and open to discussing what needs to improve, under this model, the assumption is they are most likely going to run into resistance later on.

Any motivation to start practicing a new strategy is sufficient as long as it gets people to start developing new Key Strategies. The motivation can be fear, it can be a form of conflict avoidance, or it can be a desire to please. Ideally, teams will want to cooperate and will be committed to making needed adjustments, but that is by no means a requirement for the success of the process. Any motivation to invest time and energy in trying out a new strategy works just fine.

Think about the people who need to make adjustments in your organization. How would they respond to an invitation to make adjustments? What would motivate them to try a new strategy? Ideally they will genuinely want to cooperate and learn but if not, which motivator will get them going?

....

....

....

....

Side by side with the definition of desired outcomes is the important part of assessing which strategies are needed in order for the team to achieve desired outcomes.

This first step requires great attention. It's imperative that the assessment takes into account the organizational culture, structure and dynamics, even if the goal is to change a single individual. It's imperative to define clear criteria for success and mechanisms by which the manager can identify if the needed adjustments are made and if they are sustainable.

STAGE 2: IDENTIFYING KEY STRATEGIES

At this stage, the selected strategy or strategies need to be presented to the team, however they must be presented to the team a certain very specific way that engages the EBS, not the KBS.

The strategy is first defined briefly in knowledge terms and then shown with much more attention in experience terms, through examples and case studies.

In order for teams to change, teams need to define in experience terms which strategy is required in order to meet needs or achieve desired outcomes. As I mentioned earlier, people often don't change because they literally don't see the strategies they need. To get teams to define Key Strategies in experience terms, they need to give examples of situations in which the strategy is applied. When teams don't have sufficient access to the needed strategies, their examples will initially be off, reinforcing the wrong strategy.

This is where the battle between the Knowledge Based System and the Experience Based System is most apparent. Though people understand the knowledge-based definition of the strategy, they frequently struggle with giving relevant examples of the new strategy.

Stage two is often blocked by people's inability to produce accurate examples as well as by a discomfort or an inability to think of examples in the first place.

An expert prepares the manager to overcome the pitfalls we have come to expect in each stage.

How comfortable are the people who need to make the adjustments on your team with sharing examples and telling stories? What do you anticipate will be their response to this practice?

....

....

....

....

Unlike other processes, making people feel as comfortable as possible is not a priority. In fact, making people uncomfortable before resistance has surfaced is advantageous because it accelerates the process into the third stage, which is the resistance stage. People may not follow through with the second stage for a variety of different reasons, all of which are most desirous.

A big part of preparing the manager to successfully change people focuses on allowing people to resist, making them reasonably and appropriately uncomfortable so that if there is any resistance to making a genuine investment in the needed adjustments, that resistance will surface, and the sooner the better. The only caveat here is to make sure that the resistance is directed toward discomfort with the process, not with the facilitating manager.

Completing this stage and having a new experience-based definition of a Key Strategy is often compared to what learning theories call insight learning or "A-ha" moments. It doesn't come from mimicking others or from repeating something over and over. It comes from a transformational insight that makes it possible to see things in the after version that people could not see before.

Change agents often mistakenly think that an A-ha moment is enough. It's a moment that typically feels cathartic, empowering, and deeply rewarding so it's easy to see why people think it's powerful enough to create a lasting transformation. In most cases it's not, mainly because the next stage is resistance, and it typically takes more than insight to move on and apply the needed adjustments in the face of resistance.

STAGE 3: OVERCOMING RESISTANCE

In order for teams to make needed adjustments, people need to overcome resistance to changing. We believe that 100% of people resist, but that the rare 10% of people can overcome resistance without needing external support to overcome it.

We tell our clients about a monk meditating in a room while a boy is trying to disturb him by poking him with a stick. While the monk is maintaining his meditative state, he feels and can register the disturbance, but is skilled enough to deal with it without having to stop meditating if he so chooses.

Only 10% of people can handle resistance in a way similar to the monk's response. They can deal with their own resistance effectively and quickly to the point that they can often see changing themselves as an exciting opportunity.

A word of warning here: as I discussed in earlier chapters, many teams who don't want to change will initially seem like they can change on their own. Their actions however and their lack of consistent application will prove otherwise.

The only people we include in the above 10% are those who overcome their own resistance without external support, which always results in applying the changes they agreed to apply. In our experience, this small group of people who DO want to change have somehow developed an intuitive way to go through the five stages. They have somehow intuitively figured it out often without even being aware of quickly cruising through the stages.

We believe that everyone resists changing, not just difficult individuals. Chances are people who don't want to change are everywhere around you. You can find them when you make a small request they don't follow. You'll find how wide they are spread when there are bigger adjustments needed. You'll find that people don't adopt new skills in a lasting way and will often need to learn the same lesson over and over again.

As part of the process, people will be asked to initiate a well-defined small task on a daily basis. You'll find most people will somehow not meet all the requirements of the daily task. When asked why they didn't complete the tasks, people will make a variety of different statements to explain themselves.

Suppose the people in your organization who need to make adjustments are asked to provide an example or a story a day about the required Key Strategy for several weeks. Assume they were not privy to the understanding of how telling stories about a strategy would help them achieve the goal that you hope for them to achieve.

How likely do you think they'll be to complete the daily task? (In our experience, it doesn't take more than ten minutes a day on average, but under the above conditions most people will not follow through on this daily task). What will they say when you ask them why they didn't complete the task?

Generally speaking the different responses people have fall into three categories:

→ I need more information.

→ I didn't have time, etc.

→ I don't agree with the process itself and I want to discontinue investing in the process.

The first may be genuine and not a form of resistance, or it may be a way to regain control of the process and resist. People may start with one type of response and then use the other two of course. The beauty of this process is that it's designed to overcome all three response types with great ease. Ironically, the third resistance of wanting to discontinue the process is the one we had greatest success with when it comes to changing people who don't want to change.

For most change processes, these responses can bring the process to a halt. However, the system in this book is designed to generate these responses and to equip managers to exit this third stage with relative ease. It goes without saying that there are certain things you must notice and certain things you must avoid during the resistance stage, but as a general rule, the sooner any resistance, can be surfaced and managed, the sooner your team can move on to the next needed stage.

Despite what you might think, even overcoming resistance isn't enough to guarantee lasting desired outcomes. You could work with your team to effectively define what needs to change and overcome resistance, but without the next two stages, most changes will still not sustain.

STAGE 4: CREATING SUSTAINABILITY

In order for teams to change in a lasting way, new synaptic pathways need to be sufficiently reinforced. Without sufficient and well-established reinforcement of new strategies as synaptic pathways in the brain, teams may feel motivated and enlightened but the change will typically last a few weeks before everything goes back to how things were before.

As I discussed earlier, the EBS, the system in the brain responsible for applying behavioral changes, will not adopt a new strategy until it meets certain conditions.

For a new strategy to become the new default response in the brain and affect the way people learn, plan, interact, and execute things in a lasting way, the new Key Strategy must prove, among other things, to:

→ Increase the likelihood of success
→ Apply to more situations, and
→ Have sufficient experience-related reference points

The KBS is not as selective as the EBS in this sense. Any type of information, provided it's organized in a way that the brain can understand, can be stored. The KBS can store competing knowledge and contradicting facts. It doesn't dictate choices and decisions in the same way the EBS does and hence has no need to be that selective.

The EBS is much less likely to allow adding a new strategy side by side with a well established old strategy.

I have already touched on the importance of the first two categories in the previous chapter. It takes us back to the way the new strategies are designed. Strategies that apply successfully to less situations or apply less successfully to a few situations will not make the cut. The more a strategy can be generalized to create benefits in more situations, the stronger that strategy will be, and the easier it will be to add the new synaptic pathway that represents it.

Creating reference points for using a new strategy can be

accelerated by manufacturing brain stimulated experiences so the process can take a few weeks instead of months or years. Teams differ and the number of reference points needed in order to create accurate acquisition varies by a few weeks here and there. Insufficient reference points will result in an initial application that will fade in time.

When you require the people in your organization to make needed adjustments, one of the first things that will come to mind for them will be past experiences with attempts to change.

Which type of experiences did these people have with making needed adjustments and with going through relevant change in the past?

....

....

....

....

....

People may have had frustrating experiences with other training and change processes. It's actually rare that training doesn't provide needed results because the tools and techniques taught are not relevant enough or effective enough. Most of the time, the tools and techniques are superb but people don't acquire them in a way that translates into application. Training for most people is frustrating nonetheless. The fact is most people invest time in training without having desired outcomes to justify their investment. It's not because the tools that were taught or practiced were not effective, usually it's because people are not equipped with a system that allowed them to integrate those skills into their everyday at work.

Because using the system in this book doesn't require

genuine up-front commitment, getting people to say they agree to go through the process is a more realistic task. Of course in most cases they will not truly mean they are willing to make needed adjustments up-front. That is just the natural starting point, it's almost always what you should expect. With sufficient experience-based reference points, Key Strategies will be acquired in a lasting way regardless.

STAGE 5: APPLICATION

In order for teams to change, people need to consistently turn experiences into application. Talking about changing is very different than practicing the new behaviors or changes that need to be made.

Transitioning from the fourth stage to the fifth stage is a result of translating the application of Key Strategies to a specific area. Teams who acquired KindExcellence™ can now apply it to be more assertive, for example, to achieve a specific business goal. The transition is most often natural and doesn't require further reinforcement. In this stage, teams apply the change to everything they do, building needed consistency and lasting results. Once this occurs, it's time to review the type of changes that have been applied, their connection to the original desired outcomes and if any additional Key Strategies are still needed.

Getting teams to acquire the strategies that will lead them to make needed adjustments is one of the smallest changes you can make, but its results are very impactful. Using specifically selected strategies improves performances and productivity, often echoing with increased effectiveness above and beyond the specific goals that have been originally defined.

CHAPTER 9:
TAKEAWAYS

★ The best strategies in the world, without an acquisition system, are great awareness tools that will not translate into consistent practice.

★ The five stages, the natural stages people need to go through in order to create a new synaptic pathway in the EBS are:
- Desired outcome
- Identifying Key Strategies
- Overcoming resistance
- Creating sustainability
- Application

★ Knowing the five stages allows managers to accelerate the acquisition of needed strategies.

★ The climax of this system is the third stage: overcoming resistance.

★ Initial lack of cooperation is inconsequential: you don't need to start with trust or agreement and people don't need to acknowledge they need to improve for the process to work.

★ In order for people to change, people need to define in experience terms which strategy is required in order to meet needs or achieve goals.

★ Change agents often mistakenly think that an Aha moment is enough. In most cases it's not, mainly because the next step is resistance.

★ Many people who don't want to change will initially seem like they can change on their own. Their actions however and their lack of consistent application will prove otherwise.

★ Generally speaking, the different responses people have fall into three categories:
  - I need more information.
  - I didn't have time, etc.
  - I don't like the process itself and a don't want to continue investing in the process

★ Creating reference points for using a new strategy can be accelerated by manufacturing brain stimulated experiences so the process can take a few weeks instead of months or years.

INCORPORATING BRAIN SCIENCE INTO BUSINESS SOLUTIONS

HOW CAN YOUR "CORPORATE" OR ORGANIZATIONAL BRAIN THINK FASTER?

This important question was asked by Colonel John (Richard) Boyd, a United States Air Force fighter pilot and Pentagon consultant, whose theories have been highly influential in the military, sports, and business. Boyd believed that fighter pilots didn't win because they had faster reflexes, but because their reflexes were connected to a brain that thought faster than the opponent.

The way our brains are wired is extremely important in business. A brain that is set up to learn effectively from every experience can develop to be far more successful and fast.

A brain that is programmed to follow directive rules that dictate choosing one value or one way of operating will be stagnant and much slower to identify the right solutions.

THREE OPTIONS FOR CHANGING PEOPLE

So far, getting people to change or make needed adjustments in teams has been a difficult challenge to overcome. With a few exceptions, the two options that were used in the past were too resource consuming and often fell short of delivering lasting outcomes. The new way uses the way the brain works so people can make lasting changes.

Let's go over the three ways to change people. I'll explain the challenges of the first two from a brain science perspective and then how and why the acquisition system described in Chapter Nine is so successful.

<u>OPTION A</u>: THE THERAPEUTIC MODEL:

Giving the Knowledge Based System access to Experience Based System encoding, creating awareness and then reinforcing new codes in the Experience Based System through awareness and repetition.

EBS and KBS work together in the brain. KBS is "responsible" for information and knowledge. If a boy sees his sister fall and get hurt, the boy may recall his sister's response, what she wore, what time of day it was, and the exact sequence that made her trip. All of this is information. The experience of watching his sister fall is something altogether different. The experience itself will trigger an existing or new "conclusion" or synaptic pathway. It will be generalized and with other experiences will create patterns or invisible rules that will define the way the boy engages with the world.

A therapist may ask the boy to process the rule he formed. Perhaps the boy reinforced an existing invisible rule such as:

"My sister is so clumsy" which together with other invisible rules the boy reinforced in the past, has been triggering the boy to be overprotective of her. Or maybe this was the first time the boy saw his sister fall, and that led him to form a new rule: "My sister in not as perfect as she thinks she is" which, in tandem with other existing synaptic pathways, triggered him to tease her.

The claim of traditional therapeutic approaches is that the more we can shed light on the free floating pieces of the past, turning the hidden implicit experience-based encoding into explicit, awareness-controlled knowledge-based memories, the more we can free people to live fully in the present and have new choices about how they live their lives.

In this way, therapists make codes from the EBS available for the awareness of the KBS. Once such invisible rules are brought to people's attention, therapists then draw on the high functions of awareness and attention to change the way people respond to their existing programming. In other words, therapists try to get people to use the higher functions of their cortex to calm their lower limbic-agitation.[9] Therapists would get the boy to understand the sequence that led him to tease his sister, getting the boy to change his response to his sister through awareness.

In a team setting, this would be equal to digging out the basic assumptions that are leading your team to not make needed adjustments, eliciting change though awareness. Suppose your team isn't achieving desired results because it's using less then optimal considerations for prioritizing tasks. The therapeutic model would first look to expose the faulty considerations, then, through attention and awareness, get the team motivated enough to commit to practicing the change consistently.

---

9   Dr. Daniel Siegel, Mindsight (2010), Bantam Books, P. 28

This option is a very commonly used as an application for designing change solutions in organizations. Most coaching and organizational development models are based on the therapeutic model. It's particularly difficult to achieve desired outcomes using this option in organizations for several reasons:

→ This process requires up-front cooperation and commitment, and teams often don't come into this process willingly.

→ It requires people to admit they are broken and need to be fixed, which most people will not do anyway, and in a team setting there is very little you can do to enforce.

→ With work being extremely demanding at times, attention and awareness (which are critical for the success of this model) fall victim to distractions that make it nearly impossible to maintain the effort.

→ It assumes that consciousness can overcome emotion, which is an extremely complicated adventure to get into with teams. This is especially true since organizations typically cannot devote the same amount of resources therapeutic models require in order to process feelings and emotions.

You may have noticed that for some reason the people who seem to need to change most are less likely to admit to their part, which makes coaching or otherwise using this model with teams impossible. In addition, as soon as emotions are involved, change is often blocked by the strength of resistance. When we get emotional, the middle prefrontal cortex (the region that calms the emotionally reactive lower limbic and brainstem layers) often loses the ability to regulate all the energy that's stirred up. At that point, people move directly from limbic impulse to reactive thoughts and actions.[10] Once

---

10   Dr. Daniel Siegel, Mindsight (2010), Bantam Books, P. 26

the brain is triggered, it's often extremely hard to stop this sequence. As you'll soon see, Option C prevents this sequence before it even starts.

OPTION B: THE TRAINING OR INSIGHT MODEL:

Depending on cortical consolidation to translate from the Knowledge Based System to the Experience Based System.

Knowledge from the KBS does in some cases slowly feed new encoding into the cortex in a way that affects behavior.[11] This is possible through a process I touched on briefly in early chapters called Cortical Consolidation.

It's estimated that about 2%-10% of the population can effectively translate knowledge into change. If your team left a training program with two out of ten members applying the skills and tools that were introduced, you are well familiar with this phenomenon.

Not much is known about Cortical Consolidation. It's believed to happen during sleep as information slowly interleaves into cortical networks.[12] This is a slow process and we don't know much about it yet.

In Option B, people are introduced to knowledge and experience through role-play that is designed as knowledge (we'll explore why role-play doesn't count as experience by the EBS in a moment). The expectation of this option is that people will acquire the new knowledge into experience, which is a very limiting option due to the access most people have to using Cortical Consolidation.

This two-step process (introducing knowledge to the EBS and expecting people to acquire it as experience by way of Cortical Consolidation) has consistently led to disappointing results in organizations. Some studies show that training, if combined with coaching, can reach up to 60% transference

---

11 McNaughton, 1994
12 Wilson and McNaughton, 1994, Poe et. al 2000, Louie and Wilson 2001

(where people apply the new skills in a lasting way). Without coaching, transference from training results match the 2%-10% range above.

OPTION C: KCI'S ACQUISITION SYSTEM

Engaging the Experience Based System directly, making synaptic pathways changes through directed experience.

This model doesn't depend on awareness nor does it require the involvement of Cortical Consolidation. Changes in this model are made directly to the EBS.

It's not a new model. It's the model people naturally use to create synaptic representations of invisible, subconscious rules in the first place. Children learn values by reading stories and processing morals using this model. Pilots learn to fly airplanes using this model. It's a model that has been used successfully for generations.

Engaging the EBS is an important part of managing people that most managers have no access to in business school. It initially requires an expert facilitator to guide managers through the process, helping them navigate and keep their teams on the path. However, once managers gain sufficient experience guiding people, they develop independence and can typically work to change people on their own. After some practice, managers typically only need support when it comes to extreme cases, when they themselves are involved and cannot maintain objectivity, and, of course, in identifying which strategy is required in order to achieve desired outcomes. More than anything, changing people who don't want to change is a lifelong management tool.

It's not an easy option though. The biggest challenge comes from the fact that people already have synaptic pathways in place when managers meet them. This is different than creating new synaptic pathways in childhood, when the new pathways don't contradict old existing pathways. That's where resistance comes into the picture and why knowing how to manage resistance is such a critical skill.

THE RULES OF ENGAGING THE EBS

Throughout the book we talk about the importance of engaging the EBS directly to achieve lasting change and desired outcomes. But the EBS has its own unique rules of engagement.

When people think of experience they often think of going out and doing something, but as it turns out, experience can be generated within our brain without having to move a muscle. Not everything we do is considered by the EBS as experience. The trigger that cues the creation of a new synaptic pathway can be an internal event, a thought or a feeling, or an external event that the brain associates in some way to a happening in the past.[13]

In the mid 1990s, a group of Italian neuroscientists were studying the premotor area of a monkey's cortex. As part of their experiment, they discovered that when a monkey simply watched researchers eat a peanut, the same motor neurons fired as when the monkey ate the peanut.[14] This phenomenon is associated with mirror neurons, a group of neurons that have been extensively researched in recent years.[15] The effects of watching someone else, or even a reflection people associate with themselves, doing something generates the same neural sequence that would be generated if they would have performed the action.

But, the circuits in the brain that generate experience by processing other people's experience are only activated under

---

13 Dr. Daniel Siegel, Mindsight (2010), Bantam Books, P. 148
14 Iacoboni, Mirroring People; Laurir Carr et al. *Neural Mechanisms of Empathy in Humans: A Relay from Neural Systems for Imitation of Limbic Areas*, (Proceedings of the National Academy of Sciences 100 2004)
15 V.S. Ramachandaran, 2011

very specific circumstances. If, for example, people are put in an observer role, creating dependency on the presenter to guide them through the experience, the EBS will not register that presentation as an experience. Being passively led doesn't qualify as experience. For the EBS to consider something an experience, people need to be able to initiate expectations about how the experience will move forward.

This is why when role-play is set up to mimic certain guidelines, the EBS doesn't encode it as experience either. Experiences don't have to be your own to be considered experience. You can watch someone else apply a certain maneuver and adopt it as your own. But experiences have to be self-directed[16], non-reactive, and need to happen when you voluntarily choose to focus your attention.[17]

Early on in the book, we discussed how difficult it is to change people who don't want to change and that in fact 90% of people don't want to change or seem to be unable to change. We also mentioned that there is a path, but that managers must be the guardians of that path if they are to get people to change.

Although everything in this book must fit together to change people, the rules of engaging the EBS are probably the most important to notice and manage if you are to keep your team on the above path.

There are many requirements for engaging the EBS in a way that generates new experiences and encodes them as new synaptic pathways in the brain, enough requirements to include in a separate book. Two examples, just to give you a sense of the unique language of the EBS, are the fact that the EBS only considers learner initiated experiences as "experience," and that new learning from experience will only stick if it has multiple varied reference points to build on.

---

16 Dr. Daniel Siegel, Mindsight (2010), Bantam Books, P. 41
17 Dr. Daniel Siegel, Mindsight (2010), Bantam Books, P. 39

In order for EBS to reinforce new synaptic pathways as new experiences, the examples must be generated by team members themselves. Generally speaking, the people who initiate examples encode them as experiences while those not initiating the examples will store the examples as stories told by someone else. Even if a team member initiates an example about someone else, the brain will still encode it as experience. This is why the KCI Five-Stage Acquisition System can depend on examples and accelerate the acquisition of experience that would have otherwise taken years to acquire into a short period of time.

As for creating multiple varied reference points, the EBS needs to create connections between many reference points in order for it to "see" a new experience as significant enough. The EBS harnesses the brain's capacity to generalize from experience, which is how we construct mental models from repeated patterns. The brain summarizes and combines similar events into one prototypical representation known as schema.[18]

For this reason the examples we use in order to get people to change must be from different contexts, different times, different topics, etc. Without creating multiple reference points, you'll find that many people cannot see the new strategy you are trying to introduce. You'll keep saying green and they'll keep hearing blue. Others may understand the strategy, but without multiple and varied enough reference points, the Key Strategy will only be stored in the KBS as a new insight but without the ability to apply change in a lasting way.

These and other considerations must be integrated into the way we design solutions for change.

When we started the journey to equip teams with the

---

18 Darcia Narvaez and Tonia Bock, Moral Schemas and Tacit Judgment, (Journal of Moral Education 31, no. 3, 2002)

ability to access their full potential, there were many obstacles in our way.

Individuals with great influence on the organization, often in senior positions, who needed new strategies, refused to engage in any development process. Teams nodded their heads in agreement, but were not implementing needed adjustments. Wide changes such as mergers or adopting new organizational culture were communicated by the organization's leadership without being effectively disseminated, and without reaching application in middle management, not to mention not reaching every last employee. Politics and organizational dynamics got in the way of needed changes and much more.

Our goal as change agents was to treat change like a science. We believe organizations cannot depend on a 10%-25% success of change efforts. We wanted to study change, and, in particular, changing people until we could speak of change in a predictable way.

Not everything is predictable at this point. There is a lot still to learn. Each team is different and each time we work with a team we learn something new, a better way to do things, a new slight variation to the consistent patterns we have seen over the years. We learn that there are unique features to different strategy clusters. We are continuously learning how to better equip people to use their talents and access abilities they didn't know they have. We have learned how to speed up the process considerably and how to make it extremely user-friendly, but it would be inconceivable to imagine our learning is complete.

The first step to understanding change as a science is well on its way. We have achieved consistency. We believe we can now speak of changing people, 90% of people, even teams that are highly resistant to change, in a predictable way that consistently leads to desired outcomes.

It is a gift and an honor to be a part of this process. As knowledge in brain science evolves, we are exposed to more fine-tuned explanations that can be translated into better solutions. The experience of leading thinkers, philosophers, and spiritual leaders from around the world constantly provides us with better questions. Already, the glimpse of research shared in this book as well as the research of many other scientists that are not included here, have affected many other experts in other fields, from the way diets are designed to the way medical rehabilitation is approached.

It is our hope that by bringing brain science applications to business, the huge potential of this knowledge can benefit people, not just at work but in creating healthy relationships, in families and by awakening schools to change the way they prepare students for the challenges ahead.

DIGGING DEEPER
STUDIES, RESEARCH AND RECOMMENDED READING

→ V. S. Ramachandran, *The Tell-Tale Brain: A Neuroscientist's Quest for What Makes Us Human*, W. W. Norton & Company, 2011

→ Michael S. Gazzaniga, *Who's in Charge?: Free Will and the Science of the Brain*, Ecco, 2011

→ Daniel J. Siegel, M.D. *Mindsight: The New Science of Personal Transformation*, Bantam Books, 2010

→ Olaf Sporns, *Networks of the Brain*, The MIT Press, 2010

→ Antonio R. Damasio, *Self Comes to Mind: Constructing the Conscious Brain*, Pantheon, 2010

→ Howard Gardner, *Five Minds for the Future*, Harvard Business School Press, 2009

→ Steven Pinker, *How the Mind Works*, W. W. Norton & Company, 2009

→ Jill Bolte Taylor, *My Stroke of Insight: A Brain Scientist's Personal Journey*, Viking Adult 2008

→ Norman Doidge, *The Brain That Changes Itself: Stories of Personal Triumph from the Frontiers of Brain Science,* Penguin 2007

→ Eric R. Kandel, *In Search of Memory: The Emergence of a New Science of Mind,* Norton, 2007

→ Sharon Begley, *Train Your Mind, Change Your Brain,* Random House, 2007

→ Joseph Ledoux, *Synaptic Self: How Our Brains Become Who We Are,* Penguin, 2003

→ Jeffrey M. Schwartz, M.D., Sharon Begley, *The Mind and the Brain: Neuroplasticity and the Power of Mental Force,* HarperCollins, 2002

→ John J. Ratey, *A User's Guide to the Brain: Perception, Attention, and the Four Theaters of the Brain,* Vintage, 2002

→ Eric R. Kandel, James H. Schwartz, Thomas M. Jessell, *Principles of Neural Science,* 4th edition, McGraw-Hill, 2000

→ Daniel Schacter, *Searching for Memory: The Brain, the Mind, and the Past,* Basic Books, 1996

ACKNOWLEDGEMENTS

Developing a model for changing people was one of the hardest challenges I've had to work through in my life. An ocean of knowledge and past milestones in the development of change and resistance went into the systems and models in this book. Diagnostic tools such as the Enneagram, coaching, and therapeutic models, such as NLP on one end and Cognitive Psychology on the other, have merged with philosophies like Daoism, religion knowledge, and, finally, with new science. I was often introduced to these by key people, in answer to my never ending curiosity. If it wasn't for the work of Joseph LeDoux, V. S. Ramachandran, Daniel Schacter, Daniel Siegel, Jeffrey Schwartz, Sharon Begley, Michael Gazzaniga, Jill Bolte Taylor, John Ratey, Paul Nunez, and others, making neuroscience both fascinating and accessible, the breakthrough we bring to clients probably would not have been possible.

Since the knowledge in this area is so vast, it was most difficult to choose what not to share with you so that this book doesn't turn into an academic exploration. My excitement about new research and the interconnectivity I see in everything that I included in the book could have easily blinded me. People like Robert Thele, Michael Cushman, and many others made the selection of what we now use so seamlessly with clients possible. Among many other contributions, Michael came up with the deep insight for changing people who don't want to change. He was hit by insight-lightning during what feels now like a legendary conversation with a Pakistani cab. I often wonder if the driver knew how remarkable that conversation truly was. Robert was the one who helped redesign my thinking. He mentored me and, in many ways, gave me access to my own potential.

The client cases in this book include Fortune 100 and Fortune 500 corporations, as well as smaller organizations from a large variety of industries. The names and industries were shuffled to protect their identity, but each and every case taught us something, enough to see consistent patterns. Everything we learned would have been nothing but a great theory without their leadership and I could not have done it without the brilliant Paula Farnsworth and the incredible Tanya Westby at the helm of the Key Change Institute. Special thanks go out to our senior partners and associates, Mark Herbert, Sue Stevenson, Molly Scurto, Jennifer Long, Gina Pertee, Karen Workman, Michelle Romanica , Tara Bissett, Rosie Zaldatte, Douglas Ross, Karla Brandau, Katherine Hamilton, and Dusty Meehan.

Last but not least, thanks to my family and friends. Words can hardly express my appreciation for your constant support.

ABOUT THE AUTHOR

Reut Schwartz-Hebron is the founder of the Key Change Institute (KCI), a management consulting company specializing in giving teams and organizations access to their full potential. Her interdisciplinary expertise combines brain science applications with organizational development. Over the years, Reut's solutions and principles have been successfully implemented in organizations ranging from Fortune 500s such as NIKE, Avaya, GSK, and Maconi to military units, nonprofits, and government agencies. As a consultant and speaker, she brings richness of experience working with hundreds of senior executives and teams.

Reut developed KCI's proprietary systems to emphasize the applications of experience-based learning including: KCI's Solution Assessment™, KCI's Five-Stage Acquisition System™, Extraordinary Mentoring™, and Direct Mentoring™ models.

To learn more about Reut Schwartz-Hebron and Key Change Institute's other services and products, including the institute's free resources and newsletter, please visit **www. KeyChangeNow.com**. Otherwise please join Reut on twitter and Facebook.